To D

THE AWE OF AWAKENING: A GUIDEBOOK

108 pathways
to clarity, joy
and prosperity

For the AWE

of you

Patrick's profound yet practical models undo the belief that there is something out there to be found to complete us. He helps readers quickly connect with their own heart intelligence and what it really means to be human.

—Marci Shimoff, # 1 NY Times bestselling author, *Happy for No Reason* , and *Chicken Soup for the Soul*

Every so often, I pick up a book that resonates perfectly with the tenets I know to be true. This is the case with Patrick Ryan's phenomenal book. This is definitely a must read for anyone seeking confirmation on the ideas and concepts you already support. After having read many of the great spiritual works of our time, I can honestly say that *Awakened Wisdom* is definitely among the very best.

—Dr. Peter C. Rogers author *Ultimate Truth: Book I*

Patrick is a teacher that everyone needs to know about. He shares wisdom, principles and clear action steps that will help anyone navigate the personal, professional or even global changes we are facing. You will look at yourself and your life very differently after reading *Awakened Wisdom*.

—Ariane de Bonvoisin, bestselling author of *The First 30 Days*

Patrick Ryan has taken misunderstood and misused metaphysical concepts and distilled them down to eight very practical states of being. Everyone who is on the path of discovery will benefit from *Awakened Wisdom*'s fresh and authentic approach to living a life that is congruent with their own personal brilliance.

—Mike Robbins, author of *Be Yourself, Everyone Else is Already Taken*

Awakened Wisdom gives the how to of being present in the moment that Tolle only says is possible. In a friendly, story-filled text, Ryan offers the tools to move through each moment awake. The book is a gift to those who are drawn toward the flame of full aliveness.

—David Carr, D.Div, spiritual counselor, co-leader with Laura Davis of Writer's Journey Retreats

PRAISE FOR VISION QUEST RETREATS BY PATRICK J. RYAN

Having fasted for over two days, and the pack no lighter than before, I never break my stride and never stop to rest the whole way back. The strength of the lion in me, I celebrate the clarity and the deepening of seeing my life's journey so clearly on this quest. And I am prepared for what was released to visit sometimes, but it no longer rules unidentified and powerful from the shadows. Pay attention, this is where heaven and earth meet.

—R. H., Singer/Life Coach/Broadcaster

It was a beautiful, wonderful experience and I'm absolutely pleased that I was a part of it. It isn't every day that we get the opportunity to step outside the issues of everyday life, allowing ourselves to totally immerse into the cleansing of the filters, into the connection with Spirit. —L. R., Retired Engineer

My experience of our journey in the desert was complete awakening of my heart, my body, and my mind. The opening of my heart has allowed me to be more aware and see things differently, to acknowledge and appreciate others and see the beauty of their passions.

—P. S., Corrections Retiree & Sawmill Business Owner

I have participated in many different kinds of training and development programs over the years. Most programs cover topics at a surface level. The Vision Quest drops down to the core. It's extremely personal, experiential, and transformational. I walk away clear about who I am and how I want to be in the world. I know what I am here to do. I have never felt more alive.

—K.H., Seattle WA

Other books by Patrick J. Ryan

BEST SELLER IN THE U.S. AND CANADA

Awakened Wisdom: A Guide to Reclaiming Your Brilliance

The Eagle's Call

Enjoy Patrick's blog at www.AwakenedWisdom.com for more articles.

Listen to AWE Radio on Blogtalk and at www.AwakenedWisdom.com

Learn about Awakened Wisdom Vision Quest adventures and other AWE experiences on our website at www.AwakenedWisdom.com

The AWE of Awakening

A GUIDEBOOK

108 pathways
to clarity, joy
and prosperity

PATRICK J. RYAN

Awakened Wisdom Experiences® Inc. ("AWE") is a global training, coaching and personal development organization. If you are interested in discussing the use of our proprietary materials please contact us about certification as an AWE Coach.™ AWE Coaching™ services may only be provided by certified Awakened Wisdom Experiences™ service providers.

AWE Nature™ is copyright of Awakened Wisdom Experiences. And AWE Nature Coaching(SM) is a service mark for coaching, development, educational, and training services provided by Awakened Wisdom Experiences Inc.

Published by: Awakened Wisdom
          patrick@AwakenedWisdom.com

ISBN 978-0-9842363-1-2

Cover photo by Patrick Ryan
Design and Layout by Vancouver Desktop Publishing
  Centre Ltd.

Printed by Lightning Source

The paper used in the production of this book will be offset through support for the planting of trees and other initiatives.

This book is dedicated to all

Wanderers, Wonderers, Dreamers, and
Visionaries who show up in their lives each
day willing to be Awake, Wise, and
Engaged in a good way.

And most especially, it is written for those who
step up to lead us—individuals, communities,
and world organizations—toward a more
awakened life experience.

Appreciations

I have much to appreciate in my life. There are many people and situations that have contributed to my own path of development and to the formation of Awakened Wisdom Experiences, Vision Quests, our other events, and this book.

Starting at home, appreciation goes to my amazing wife, companion, and friend Mary Diamond, who always provides love, support, insight, and unquestioning resolve in her encouragement toward the work that I am called to.

To Ginny Joyce, executive coordinator of Awakened Wisdom, who cares for the space and all other things of Awakened Wisdom. She leads us forward with generosity, good effort, and her own wisdom.

To Mary Agnes Antonopoulos, who has selflessly offered her wisdom on the perplexing world of social media.

To Ann West whose gentle and brilliant editing touches have brought the quality of this offering to a higher level.

To Amy Egenberger, who has provided insight and courage to the AWE experience in countless ways.

To the many AWE volunteers and supporters who have organized events, talks, and conferences all around the world. I am in AWE of you all.

To my Sayadaw, my master, teacher, and guide through the Burmese experience. He provided the opportunity for me to find my own way to realizations that have reshaped my being and my entire worldview.

To White Eagle, Wind Eagle, Rainbow Hawk, and my Indonesian, Burmese, Malay, Mexican, and Indian guides, who have supported me in the shattering. Blessings.

Appreciation as well to the courageous ones who join us for our Vision Quests, Wisdom Circles, and coaching events. Your stories inspire me every day.

And appreciation to all the amazing humans who embrace the opportunity to grow and develop yourselves for the well-being of us All. You are all the light of this work and this world.

Contents

Welcome

This book leads to a deepening of the Eight States of an Awakened Life,© which I introduced in *Awakened Wisdom: A Guide to Reclaiming Your Brilliance.*

The AWE of Awakening uses the Eight States as a meditative contemplation with updated verses and reflection for each, followed by an inquiry and suggested practice.

This is intended to be a guidebook to support you in creating your own living practice. As always, I encourage you to take from my interpretation what works and to leave what does not.

The guidebook presents 108 verses, a mystical number in many traditions. There are typically 108 beads on a string of meditation beads, one for each possibility of realizing the truth of existence.

I resonate mostly with the understanding that 108 represents the One (1), the No-thing (0), and everything, Infinity (8)—all three are the ultimate Reality of this Universe.

May these 108 offerings guide you in creating your own amazing life journey.

Getting Started

Though greatness does happen at times through virtuous accident, it is more often aspired to and earned through good intention, effort, and action.

No book can do your work for you. You must have your own direct experience. Living a life in which you are awake, wise, and engaged is a day-by-day practice of making aware choices and responding to what life presents as you journey along.

This book reflects a process of deep meditation, informed by my own experience over the years as an entrepreneur. It is also strongly influenced by my experience as a Buddhist monk in Burma (Myanmar) as well as by teachings I have been given from a variety of beautiful and generous wisdom teachers around the world.

As we all raise the quality of our awareness together, the world will shift accordingly.

Patrick J. Ryan, Founder
www.AwakenedWisdom.com

How to Use This Book

There is no right way to use a guidebook such as this. As always, trust your own wisdom in choosing what will support you in getting the most out of it.

You could open to any page randomly, using synchronicity to guide you through it.

You could choose one of the Eight States that you are curious about or that you would like to work on more in your life. Then follow the verses of that state and notice what shifts.

You could just start reading from the beginning and then stop at some point, landing on a verse or practice assignment that resonates for you.

What is important is that you take in the spirit of the words, walk with the inquiries, and practice according to your own wisdom. In that way, you will have your own awareness—the Awakened Wisdom Experience Way, the AWE Way.

The Eight States

Each of the Eight States of an Awakened Life is presented in its own chapter. Each chapter begins with an overview of verses that interpret the various ways this state points us toward living an awakened life. Each verse is then presented on its own page for a deeper experience.

The 108 verse offerings are structured as follows, starting at the top of each page:

State
Each of the Eight States is named at the top of the page so you can know on which dimension you are working.

Verse
Each page features one verse from the corresponding state. The verse could be a meditation to consider with or without reading the rest of the page.

Reflection
Following each verse, I offer own reflection or context for what that verse points us to consider. Feel free to create your own understanding of what this verse is offering you.

Inquiry

You will find an inquiry for you to ponder throughout the day. As you do, notice any insight that occurs to you. Next, release that insight as one possibility and return to walking with the question.

Practice

Each page offers a practice suggestion. It is only a suggestion as your own wisdom may inspire you to a more relevant way to practice the offering of that page.

Reading these ideas is good. Learning these ideas is better. Experiencing the teachings of this book through each day and expanding your awareness is the way to transformation.

Eventually, with practice, the Eight States become integrated into who you are being. They are expressed through what you are doing as you walk your moment-by-moment walk both personally and professionally.

That is the Awakened Wisdom Experience Way.

Some Ideas to Gather Around

Here are some brief descriptions of several concepts in this book. They are intended to support you in a quick and good start. You will recognize these ideas and may have your own terms to describe them.

While using this guidebook, you are invited to assume a beginner's mind. Step into an empty space so that you may experience the ideas, verses, inquiries, and practices with openness, curiosity, and the humility of a hungry learner.

AWE Nature™

When you are connected to the One in you that is present, engaged, clear, grounded, wise, resourceful, flexible, value-based, creative, visionary, appreciative, generous, and kind, you are connected to your AWE Nature. Your AWE Nature is open to the interrelatedness of All, to Unity, and to the Wisdom Field.

Through AWE Nature, you are Awake, Wise, and Engaged.

Awake is being present, in the moment of now. It also includes noticing cleanly and clearly the situation of this moment.

Wise is being able to access wisdom that goes beyond your intellect and experience. Such wisdom is available through your heart, mind, and body by attuning to the Wisdom Field.

Engaged includes accepting that you are the self-authority and author of your life. It means being willing to activate your wisdom, intentions, words, and action in a good way according to your own wisdom.

Distorted Self

Essentially, distorted self is that aspect of you that gets caught in untruths. Untruths include exaggerating, diminishing, or withholding what is.

Distortions create the illusion of separation. Your self gets caught in fear, doubt, judgment, and procrastination, absorbed in criticizing, shaming, and blaming. Other distortions are aversions, attractions, or attachments that run your life and undermine your true Self.

Observer

You have the capacity to develop a reliable Observer. Through practice, you can activate the Observer within so you may gather the facts of any situation in which you find your Self.

The Observer's report does not include opinions about what is observed. It is simply a noticing of what can be observed and reported as factually as possible. With practice you can get a report on your internal state—how you are emotionally, mentally, and physically—as well as what is happening in the world around you.

Ego

For the purpose of this book, ego is any sense of "I am." Ego is not good or bad. It is necessary to function as a human in this world. For ultimate spiritual liberation, however, we want to be free from identifications of the ego.

"I am" provides reference points for the ego to exist, such as you versus me; we and them; here and there; and past, present, future. These also can lead to distortions and separation.

Wisdom Portals of Mind, Body, and Heart

Obviously you have a mind, body, and heart. Beyond the physical function of the brain, physical body, and active heart and lungs, there is a realm of wisdom associated with each body center.

The three wisdom portals are so intertwined that one can find no absolute separation among them. They operate as a unified source of wisdom and direct experience.

Still, it can be helpful to discuss these portals individually to learn about them and develop greater access to each one. We tend to specialize in one portal primarily, access one as a backup or Plan B, and push one of the three further away. Through awareness and personal development, you may learn to access and integrate all three.

Mind accesses memories and creates stories. It also assesses, plans, analyzes, and perceives. In each second, your mind perceives far more information than anyone could be aware of. When the mind notices something dangerous or important in some way, it pulls one's attention to whatever that is.

When you are accessing your AWE Nature, your mind is open, clear, and able to process and interpret a deeper wisdom. This wisdom goes beyond intellect, beyond your learned knowledge base, and even beyond your capacity to arrive at an idea through reason alone.

Body holds its own memories, such as muscle and emotional memory, beyond the obvious physical level. The body is also highly attuned to its surroundings. Have you felt the hair on your arm or the back of your neck stand up in response to something you might not otherwise be aware of?

We commonly refer to a gut feeling as sensing more to a situation than meets the eye. This could also lead to stressing our muscles or even generating some illness. These are just the body's way of getting our attention when sensing something it wants us to be aware of.

Heart includes your relational experience in the world in addition to the beating of the heart and the breathing function of the lungs. When you fall in love, your heart opens fully. When you get afraid, your heart closes off. When you are connected to your AWE Nature, you are open, receptive, and intuitive. The heart portal is able to intuit energies, insights, and information within the Wisdom Field.

Wisdom Field

There is a type of energy that runs through and among All. This phenomenon is referred to as the collective consciousness or the field. We use aspects of this field to experience the insights we call intuition. When you are thinking of someone and she calls in just that moment, you are having a field experience. The field includes many qualities and levels of energy, thought, and emotions to which we all contribute.

If we reside in distorted self, we get caught in fear and isolation, thereby cutting ourselves off from the Wisdom Field.

By activating our intention to attune to the wisdom within the field, we have access to resourcefulness, creativity, and insight far beyond what can be explained as intellect, memory, or reason. To expand access, it helps to be as open and clear as possible, like we are when connected to our AWE Nature.

The Eight States of an Awakened Life™

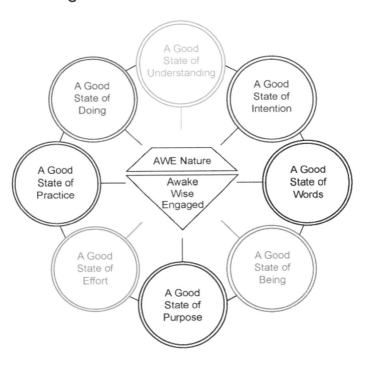

A Good State of Understanding

VERSE 1

I understand that All and I are interrelated, and as such we are One.

VERSE 2

I seek understanding.

VERSE 3

I am infinite consciousness; I am the sweeper of the broom; I am the mirror; I am you; I am who I aspire to be; I am the inspired and the inspiration.

VERSE 4

I understand that as a human, I aspire, learn, grow, and develop throughout this human journey and that there is no such destination as perfection or finished.

VERSE 5

I understand that we are all part of the Wisdom Field.

VERSE 6

I understand that the true nature of this Universe is diversity. I respect the value of the full range of beings, things, and ideas that make up the wholeness of this Universe.

VERSE 7

I understand that my expectations, intentions, and words are powerful tools of creation.

VERSE 8

I understand that I am my own healer. The healing and balancing activity of my mind, body, and heart is a constant process.

VERSE 9

I understand that what I believe to be absolutely true becomes true because I believe it. Therefore, I understand that holding a question is more useful than grasping an answer.

VERSE 10

I understand that I am the self-authority of the whole of my life, and it is through my choices that I author the unfolding adventure.

VERSE 11

I understand that All is energy, that energy just is, and that energy is transformed according to the intentions of my thoughts, words, and actions.

VERSE 12

I understand that I create my own karma. Every intention, thought, word, or action has an impact, and every impact has a consequence for which I am responsible.

VERSE 13

I understand that we are learning and developing through this life, and so I meet us All with generosity, compassion, and good intention.

VERSE 14

I understand that all people, beings, things, and circumstances are impermanent and there is a natural cycle and timing to All. Thus, the opportunity of each moment is to be present, for past and future live only as story or dream, and the moment of now is where all is One.

VERSE 15

I understand the Law of Attraction: whatever I put my expectation and intention on is what I will create in my life. I am in a dance with the Universe. What I call in, therefore, will be in accordance with the larger unfolding picture of All.

VERSE 16

I understand that this Universe is generous in its nature, abundant in possibilities, and filled with all the resources that all beings and I need.

I am in a Good State of Understanding.

VERSE 1

I understand that All and I are
interrelated, and as such we are One.

REFLECTION

The single greatest illusion is that we are in any
way separate from each other or from any situation in this world. In love, you forget the sense of
otherness and find your Self in Oneness. In the
depths of your greatest struggles, in exhaustion
there may be a shattering of ego. Separation dis-
solves; there is no-thing left but love. Confronted
by nature's beauty, you find your Self breathless,
inspired, your heart opened in awe. It is normal for
your ego to be afraid of losing its illusion of indi-
viduality, of being hurt or disappointed, and even
to doubt that such beauty happened at all. But it
did. And, it awoke a yearning deep within that will
not go back to sleep.

INQUIRY

What is needed to open to love?

PRACTICE

Notice when you push away from another
person or a situation that is in your life.

Are you willing to open
your heart to this One?

Follow through with action
inspired by wisdom.

I seek understanding.

REFLECTION

When conflict arises, whether it is with family, community, or colleagues or across the divide of religion, politics, and nations, fear gets activated. It is so easy and natural to lock onto what you know—your truth, what you believe happened and why. As you do, you shut off the possibility of another perspective or explanation. Being right becomes more important than growth and learning. Scarcity and the fear of loss run the conversation and the behavior. Distorted self activates right or wrong, win or lose, them or us; it insists that the other change. AWE Nature opens heart and mind; gets curious, flexible, willing; appreciates differences, multiple possibilities, resourcefulness; and activates possibilities and abundance energy.

INQUIRY

What do I need to stay open?

PRACTICE

Where is your mind made up, your heart closed?

Choose to activate listening, curiosity, and learning.

VERSE 3

I am infinite consciousness; I am the
sweeper of the broom; I am the mirror;
I am you; I am who I aspire to be; I am
the inspired and the inspiration.

REFLECTION

We humans are the lens between the infinite Oneness and the duality of existing. When we are
grounded, open, at One, and in love, we may, when
we least expect it, slip through a crack in time and
have a direct experience of no-other. Then return
we must to function in our human form. We necessarily move about as embodied ego–thinking,
sensing, witnessing other. We are consciousness
looking back at Self.

INQUIRY

If anything were possible, then what?

PRACTICE

Notice your present condition. Are you
open, free, in love?
Or constricted, afraid, caught in fear?

Do one act of kindness and generosity.

I understand that as a human, I aspire,
learn, grow, and develop throughout this
human journey and that there is no such
destination as perfection or finished.

REFLECTION

This too shall pass. All is impermanent. Nothing
is exempt from this truth. Nothing is static, done,
finished. We are all on a continuous path of development. This beautiful condition keeps the world
vibrant, changing, growing. Happiness passes; so
too does suffering. We are able to engage in this
process through our dreaming, visioning, and
aspiring. These practices engage us and activate
our journey. The path is as uncertain as the outcome. All we need do is to embrace the inevitabil-
ity of suffering, love life, engage happily, and give
our Self over to the extraordinary experience of
being human.

INQUIRY

What is my opportunity in this life?

PRACTICE

Create a vision board; engage your
willing heart and open mind to
allow any inspiration to appear.

VERSE 5

I understand that we are all
part of the Wisdom Field.

REFLECTION

Have you ever had a profound insight?

Or thought of someone who appeared or called
out in that moment?

Or had a great idea for a new invention or service
and someone else announced the same thing?

Or experienced an intuition to do something, and
you did, and something amazing came from it?

Or ignored a hunch only to experience trouble
because you did not act?

These are Wisdom Field experiences.

Through thoughts, words, and actions you contribute to the Wisdom Field. Open your heart,
mind, and body to listen.

INQUIRY

What intuition wants my attention?

PRACTICE

Go for a walk in nature or a nearby park.

Notice a butterfly, a bird, a person,
a leaf that blows by. Imagine there
is learning in this encounter. Journal
what learning this event offers.

I understand that the true nature of this
Universe is diversity. I respect the value of
the full range of beings, things, and ideas that
makeup the wholeness of this Universe.

REFLECTION

In this amazing hoop of life, all beings have a place, contribution, or reason for being. Nature is exquisite in her wisdom of the Circle. All belong! Our bodies are made of minerals, plants, and beings that are of the earth. In this way, we are earth consciousness embodied as humans. We may be the only beings on earth who have the capacity to receive and imagine a dream, a vision, a future world—and then go create it. We are able to represent All aspects of the Universe in our dream. In fact, the dream itself may be given from the Universe. We humans have nothing to fear in this.

INQUIRY

What is my gift in diversity?

PRACTICE

Gather pictures of plants, animals,
insects, oceans, forests, a wide variety
of people and all beings, planets, and
stars. Create a collage of the Universe.

I Am in a Good State of Understanding

I understand that my expectations, intentions, and words are powerful tools of creation.

REFLECTION

Every thought, word, or action to which we give energy is a creative force. As we journey through life, we develop a story about how the world works. This sets up our expectations, which often operate below the level of consciousness. We create intentions consciously according to what we want to experience. Often our expectations are not aligned with our intentions. You could go into a job interview saying you will get the job while still not expecting to. It follows that we can harness the creative energy of our intentions and words even more by releasing old stories and unhelpful expectations.

INQUIRY

What are my underlying expectations?

PRACTICE

Notice when your underlying expectations are not congruent with your intentions.

Choose to release the old story of expectations.

I understand that I am my own healer. The healing and balancing activity of my mind, body, and heart is a constant process.

REFLECTION

Having a healthy body, mind, and heart begins with your willingness to love your Self unconditionally. Your state of well-being and balance results from a continuous process of moment-by-moment choices. Make poor choices of diet, exercise, and care and you will live the consequences. How is the resistance serving you? If you are knowingly making poor choices, it is because you are getting something from them. Honestly, what are you really choosing? Regardless of your past, anything is possible. A great future begins with a loving present.

INQUIRY

What if I am worth it?

PRACTICE

Get connected to your AWE Nature and assess where the opportunities are to improve well-being. You are responsible for the choices and quality of your own journey. Ask for help.

VERSE 9

I understand that what I believe to be absolutely
true becomes true because I believe it.
Therefore, I understand that holding a question
is more useful than grasping an answer.

REFLECTION

Your beliefs make things appear real, solid, and
no longer flexible. Sometimes this can support
you. When you get out of bed in the morning and
believe in gravity, your feet land on the floor. Your
belief in gravity supports you. Other beliefs may
not. If you believe that relationships are hard, you
will collect evidence to support this belief. Answers
become beliefs. Curiosity creates possibilities. An
open mind and heart are flexible.

INQUIRY

To be happy, what do I need to risk?

PRACTICE

Notice an underlying assumption or belief.

Go out today and ask people how the
opposite could be true. You might say,
"Tell me about how relationships are easy."

Notice your own willingness or resistance to the
possibility of another perspective. Listen openly.

I understand that I am the self-authority of
the whole of my life, and it is through my
choices that I author the unfolding adventure.

REFLECTION

You are the author, the authority, and the storyteller of your life. You write and create your story with each choice you make and through each
telling of your story. Is AWE Nature or distorted
self your storyteller? Have you cast yourself as the
victim or the heroine? Even though embraced by
AWE Nature, you may sometimes find all the good
choices difficult, but at least you have choices. You
may choose to love your Self, to accept your birthright to happiness.

INQUIRY

As the author of my life, what will I create today?

PRACTICE

As the lead character in your life stories, are you
being truthful, respecting your Self and others?

If not, then activate your AWE Nature and
rewrite your story, freed from needing to be right
or wrong and willing to learn in a good way.

I Am in a Good State of Understanding

I understand that All is energy, that
energy just is, and that energy is
transformed according to the intentions
of my thoughts, words, and actions.

REFLECTION

We know that everything is energy. Energy takes a variety of forms, such as a wave or particle, a solid, liquid, or gas. Energy cannot be created or destroyed. It is available to be transformed. Your intentions lead the transformation of energy to form. Your words are waveforms of creative potential. Your actions are energy in motion. The energy of any person or situation is subject to being shifted by you. What will you shift it to? Love is energy; fear is energy. Love is far more powerful and sustainable than fear. It takes courage to choose love.

INQUIRY
Will I choose love today?

PRACTICE
Imagine the kind of world
you would love to live in.

Identify five things you can do to
shift a situation you are in to be
more congruent with your vision.

Choose actions from that list and follow through.

I Am in a Good State of Understanding

I understand that I create my own karma.
Every intention, thought, word, or action
has an impact, and every impact has a
consequence for which I am responsible.

REFLECTION

Happiness generates happiness; anger creates more anger. Joy is like a breeze that lifts all it touches; rage destroys. In each moment, these are all choices of ways to respond to a person or situation. Each choice has a corresponding impact—instant karma. You may say or do something that creates a mess, upset, or another unintended reaction. Congratulations on your humanness. Now go clean it up and turn that situation into love.

INQUIRY
What is my impact?

PRACTICE
Notice the impact of your behavior.

Are you creating beauty and providing life-giving energy to those with whom you engage?

Experiment with new behaviors in which you see opportunity for improvement.

VERSE 13

I understand that we are learning
and developing through this life,
and so I meet us All with generosity,
compassion, and good intention.

REFLECTION

I have made many mistakes in my life. I have said things that unintentionally caused hurt; I have done things that went wrong; and I have gone against my intuition and wisdom, living some consequences as a result. Through it all I have grown, learned, developed. I am sure that you have your own story of events not turning out as you wanted. This is life. The opportunity is to learn from successes and failings, to stay open, to be compassionate with yourself and others, and to take good risks. Your distorted self might conclude that risks are not worth the pain. That is a natural conclusion but not one that supports creating a life of dreams, growth, and prosperity.

INQUIRY

What dream is worth the risk?

PRACTICE

Where are you playing it safe?

Make a courageous choice to stay or to leap.

VERSE 14

I understand that all people, beings, things,
and circumstances are impermanent and there
is a natural cycle and timing to All. Thus, the
opportunity of each moment is to be present,
for past and future live only as story or dream,
and the moment of now is where all is One.

REFLECTION

The memories of the past fade and shift; the hopes
and dreams for the future are not yet made real.
The seasons come and go; your breath rises and
falls; your heart beats, then rests and beats again. A
day of rest followed six days of creation. A baby is
born, becomes a child, a youth, an adult, a parent,
and an elder—and then dies. Every cycle is filled
with opportunity. Who you are in relationship to
the cycle and timing of a situation asks something
different of you.

INQUIRY

What is passing through my life today?

PRACTICE

Notice where you may be resisting a change.
Become aware of what you are holding
onto. What does this change ask of you?
Choose and follow through as needed.

VERSE 15

I understand the Law of Attraction:
whatever I put my expectation and
intention on is what I will create in
my life. I am in a dance with the
Universe. What I call in, therefore,
will be in accordance with the
larger unfolding picture of All.

REFLECTION

We humans are amazing creators. We dream it;
we build it. When your expectations, intentions,
words, and actions are aligned, much is possible.
When you are aligned with what is being asked by
the world around you, then anything is possible.
The world has a dream that is emerging, and you
are called to play your part in it. Each moment
holds all potential. The outcome is not personal;
it is just as you think. Attune your listening to the
Wisdom Field. What part are you being called to
play? Align this call to your genius.

INQUIRY
What part will I play today?

PRACTICE
Ask three people about what genius you carry.

VERSE 16

I understand that this Universe is generous in
its nature, abundant in possibilities, and filled
with all the resources that all beings and I need.

REFLECTION

Look out at the stars; look within through a
microscope. Either way, you will experience infinity.
This is the abundance of All. It just is. Scarcity is
an illusion; embrace the truth that all is available.
When you are inspired with a vision, just get going.
All you need is within you. Activate your courage
and move according to your wisdom. Stay open to
support along the way. Your commitment creates
commitment in others, reducing any risk. Hesi-
tation creates more reasons to be afraid; courage
creates opportunity.

INQUIRY
What dream could be?

PRACTICE
Let the world in. Give voice to and
share your vision, your inspiration.

Support others in accordance
with your talent and genius.

A Good State of Intention

I am in a Good State of Intention.

VERSE 17
I am open and responding to the call, today's expression of my being, and I develop myself willingly to be what I am.

VERSE 18
My intention is informed by my dream, vision, and purpose. It is in resonance with my own wisdom as inspired through my heart-mind-body connection to the Wisdom Field.

VERSE 19
I meet all others and myself with love, generosity, and compassion. I create a respectful space for our commonality and diversity, for well-being and the wholeness in which we are One.

VERSE 20
I meet the challenge of obstacles and opportunities that appear along my path with the intention of learning, growing, appreciating, and loving all that shows up.

VERSE 21
From a Good State of Intention, my thoughts arise. This stream of consciousness carries beauty and life-giving energy out to all beings who are touched by her waters.

VERSE 22

I notice each thought as it arises and choose whether or not to encourage it, feed it, fan its embers. If through discernment I decide that a thought does not add beauty or is not life giving, I release it.

VERSE 23

My intentions burn bright with love and the willingness to be generous with my time, effort, and resources to all beings and myself.

VERSE 24

I am tolerant and curious with those I do not understand. I am also compassionate with the fearful, judgmental, doubtful aspects of myself. I realize that any sense of other, or separation, is of my own making. Therefore, I hold the intention and willingness to remove any veils of separation that exist as I touch into the Oneness, which we all are.

I am in a Good State of Intention.

I am open and responding to the call,
today's expression of my being, and I
develop myself willingly to be what I am.

REFLECTION

Inspiration sparks vision. Now stirred, I must say yes or no. If I say yes, I am then on a new adventure, called to create possibly without a map, resources, or instruction. . .but with willingness to put my life on the line. Analysis grips my mind; fear approaches my heart. My body tenses in response to the risk, the cessation of comfort and loss of feeling safe. Some of this concern is informed by wisdom, now caught in distorted agenda for safety's sake. I shake off the fear; the call is more important than my smallness. I respond through my AWE Nature, and wisdom kicks in. First, I must BE that. I tell myself and the world that as of today I am a _____. Some turn away; some turn toward. I move forward one breath, one step, one day.

INQUIRY

What is more important than playing safe?

PRACTICE

If you are called to be something, own it now.

VERSE 18

My intention is informed by my dream, vision, and purpose. It is in resonance with my own wisdom as inspired through my heart-mind-body connection to the Wisdom Field.

REFLECTION

Wisdom is available to you when you are willing to listen to your intuition (heart), perceptions (mind), and senses (body). All you have to do is to stay open to love, listen deeply, and respond courageously. Wisdom reveals itself in dreams, where many beings pass by, interrelated through the subtle realms of light and sound. Dreams inspire your vision and invite you to the dance of life as embodied, sensual spirit. You are a silk thread in the spiral fabric of the whole Universe. Your genius is part of the grand design. Activate the energy of your AWE Nature, attune to your wisdom, and enjoy. Move! Now is the time to say yes.

INQUIRY

What intention inspires my dance today?

PRACTICE

Choose to activate your AWE Nature today.

I meet all others and myself with love, generosity, and compassion. I create a respectful space for our commonality and diversity, for well-being and the wholeness in which we are One.

REFLECTION

Many cultures hold that as two humans meet, the highest One is coming through each of them. The wisest, most reverent, beautiful being is said to have entered the room and, in this moment, nothing is more important. The best manners are activated and generosity abounds, for what would you withhold from One so exalted? Joy emanates as hearts open and minds are hungrily poised. There is great possibility that something will be learned from this auspicious event. Through the eyes of each One present, the view of the other is of this elevated nature.

INQUIRY

How will I prepare for such a meeting today?

PRACTICE

Move through this day with the humility of One who walks among great teachers.

I meet the challenge of obstacles and
opportunities that appear along my path
with the intention of learning, growing,
appreciating, and loving all that shows up.

REFLECTION

Life will challenge us often. This situation is not
personal; it is seldom a sign. It is just normal in the
course of a life well lived. You can see challenge as
an opportunity or an obstacle; either way, it is a
mirror of your Self. You could get afraid, doubtful,
critical, or judgmental, which would be normal
for many. Or, you could be courageous, resourceful, and kind to those around you. All are viable
choices that will create corresponding experiences
and karma. Meet life as a learner with appreciation
and love.

INQUIRY

What do I appreciate about today's challenges?

PRACTICE

Notice your habits as you meet life's challenges.
Choose love or fear, resourcefulness or doubt.
Through every choice you will learn and grow.

From a Good State of Intention, my thoughts
arise. This stream of consciousness carries
beauty and life-giving energy out to all
beings who are touched by her waters.

REFLECTION

Intention shapes your energy much as a lens can
focus light. The quality of light you shine affects
everyone around. Intention also moves ambiguity
to the side. The clearer you are, the easier it is for
the Universe and others to support you. Include
creating beauty through your thoughts, words,
and actions as part of your intention.

INQUIRY

What impact will I choose to have today?

PRACTICE

Before each encounter with others today,
choose not just what you want to accomplish
but also what kind of experience you wish to
create. During your meetings, you could create
pessimism or hopefulness, worry or inspiration,
panic or peace. Any of these are valid choices.

I Am in a Good State of Intention

VERSE 22

I notice each thought as it arises and choose
whether or not to encourage it, feed it,
fan its embers. If through discernment
I decide that a thought does not add
beauty or is not life giving, I release it.

REFLECTION

Thoughts arise. At the moment a thought arises,
it is just a thought. First, activate your Observer.
Notice the quality of each thought and choose
whether to give it more energy or not. Notice and
then choose wisely. Consider if your thought is
creating beauty and generating life-giving energy.
If it is, this is likely a thought worth expanding. If
not, then simply release it with appreciation and
without judgment.

INQUIRY

What would my world be like if my thoughts
carried beauty and life-giving energy out to all?

PRACTICE

Notice your pattern. Do you tend toward
distortions such as criticism or judgment,
or toward possibilities, love, and appreciation?
Choose a life-giving habit. Practice your choice.

My intentions burn bright with love and the willingness to be generous with my time, effort, and resources to all beings and myself.

REFLECTION

This is an abundant Universe. You may be constricting under the pressure of too much to do. It often feels real, yet it is an illusion. The world presents a drumbeat it wants you to follow. It is a trance dance asking you to fit in. Trust your own wisdom. Do not be a victim to the circumstances of the world. Become the leader of what is possible. When you are critical of yourself or another, breathe and send love and appreciation. When you feel especially busy, give your time. When scarcity creeps in, open up and share happily and easily.

INQUIRY

In what way can I be more generous?

PRACTICE

Notice any situation in which you have felt frustration, anger, judgment, or disagreement.

Send thoughts of appreciation and loving-kindness to both yourself and others involved.

VERSE 24

I am tolerant and curious with those I do not understand. I am also compassionate with the fearful, judgmental, doubtful aspects of myself. I realize that any sense of other, or separation, is of my own making. Therefore, I hold the intention and willingness to remove any veils of separation that exist as I touch into the Oneness, which we all are.

REFLECTION

It is easy to be open with people and situations you like, agree with, or relate to. The big move is to experience appreciation, love, and kindness when people and situations seem opposed, scary, threatening, or unimportant—whatever judgment you throw up between you. Fear is the judge, the critic. Choose appreciation, curiosity, and listening as bridge-building skills.

INQUIRY

What do I appreciate about _____?

PRACTICE

Listen and get curious when you experience judgment. Release any agenda saying you and another must agree. Look for what you can appreciate and listen, listen, listen.

I Am in a Good State of Intention

A Good State of Words

I am in a Good State of Words.

VERSE 25

Sound creates transformation. I am the instrument of sound through tones, hymns, chants, affirmations, prayer, song, and words—according to the wisdom of my AWE Nature.

VERSE 26

I tell stories as this day's expression of who I am, allowing my state of wholeness to be beyond description.

VERSE 27

My words are informed by the inspiration, vision, and dream of the Universe's call; they resonate with the One heartbeat.

VERSE 28

My words are created from my Good State of Intention; therefore, my speech creates beauty and more life.

VERSE 29

My words honor all those around me, including myself.

VERSE 30

My words reflect my inner state of being.

VERSE 31

My words create positive effects on those who hear them and those about whom I speak.

VERSE 32

My words are not used as a weapon against others or myself.

VERSE 33

My words evoke creativity, generosity, appreciation, and good action.

VERSE 34

My words are carried by breath, which blows encouragement onto the embers of possibility for others and myself.

VERSE 35

My words are spoken cleanly in challenging situations, and I listen, listen, listen.

VERSE 36

My words give life to what desires to be born and completion to what is ready to let go.

VERSE 37

My words are truthful, kind, and needed.

I am in a Good State of Words.

Sound creates transformation. I am the instrument of sound through tones, hymns, chants, affirmations, prayer, song, and word—according to the wisdom of my AWE Nature.

REFLECTION

Many mythological stories tell us how breath, sound, and words activated creation or destruction. Today, sonic waves are used everywhere from building construction to dentistry. Have you ever been transported out of your mind by the angelic tones of a song, hymn, or chant? Music soothes, inspires, rallies, quiets, and moves us in so many ways. Great speeches have reshaped the world and created history in accordance with the speaker's intentions. As you engage with others, take the opportunity to create a shift in yourself and everyone else who comes within range of your sound.

INQUIRY

What impact do I intend through my sound?

PRACTICE

Choose and listen to music that aligns with your intention and activity. Use your voice consciously.

I tell stories as this day's expression
of who I am, allowing my state of
wholeness to be beyond description.

REFLECTION

There are no words, paragraphs, or books that could ever be written to come close to conveying the wholeness of You. Any attempt to define your Self, such as "I am _____," would fall short. Nevertheless, your description would be partially true. If you said "I am happy," for example, I would know you are in touch with happiness, and if we dropped into conversation, I would likely find that you are also sad, or frustrated, or hurt. All of this is true at the same time. It is helpful to allow for the wholeness of your experience through your use of words.

INQUIRY
Who am I? And what else?

PRACTICE
Practice this inquiry as a meditation.

My words are informed by the inspiration,
vision, and dream of the Universe's call;
they resonate with the One heartbeat.

REFLECTION

In a world of you versus me, them or us, win or
lose, fear and scarcity, it is natural that you would
take what you want, push yourself up on the backs
of others, or duck, keeping your head low for fear
of getting hurt. In that world, it is okay to accomplish goals and objectives at the expense of others or the planet. There is another world where
each person brings genius to the table; we gather around, each of us called to bring our best. Together, we imagine the hologram of our dream, in
which we each have the wholeness of it yet play our
individual part. There is abundant energy for All.
Each of these realities is equally available now.

INQUIRY

What is your part in the Universe's dream?

PRACTICE

In conversation, writing, song, or other
forms, express the words for your calling.

My words are created from my Good
State of Intention; therefore, my
speech creates beauty and more life.

REFLECTION

Your intentions inform your words. Your words could be creating beauty and providing life-giving energy if you would add that to your intention. Your true intention will affect your choice of words, the tone of how they are delivered, and their impact. When I was a monk in Burma, often another monk would invite me to join in some activity. He would ask, "Would you like to walk with me happily?" or, "Would you join me for this ceremony sincerely?" Adding the words happily or sincerely called me to a higher level of consciousness, choice, and awareness.

INQUIRY
What will my words create today?

PRACTICE
Are your intentions, words, and tone congruent?

Choose words according to the
experience you wish to create.

I Am in a Good State of Words

My words honor all those around me, including myself.

REFLECTION

We are all amazing, gifted, beautiful human beings. It is everyone's birthright to be happy, fulfilled, generous, and kind. It is common for your ego to learn survival strategies, such as putting yourself or another down or up, or complaining, judging, criticizing. Speaking well of some and poorly of others are acts of fear through distorted ego. These are acquired habits. It is love that frees us from struggle and pain. Words can create separation or bring us together. You are now ready for the opportunity of conscious language. Be the source of creating respect for All. As you speak, it shall be. Shift your word habit into one that honors yourself and others. Speak words of appreciation for yourself, family, colleagues, and strangers.

INQUIRY

Who will my words honor today?

PRACTICE

Express appreciation to the people you meet today. Expect nothing in return.

I Am in a Good State of Words

My words reflect my inner state of being.

REFLECTION

The ancient Greeks gifted us with the aphorism "First, know thyself." It is helpful to acknowledge the big challenge: we experience ourselves only subjectively. Further, we are often invested in being viewed a particular way: smart, together, accomplished, desirable, or in contrast, unreliable, lazy, unattractive, and so on. We then seek and collect evidence for how we want to be seen. Developing a reliable Observer is one way to take in a cleaner reflection of your state of being. Your behavior, words, and choices are a mirror for your internal reality. Notice. To navigate out of the forest, it is helpful to know where you are now and to what state of growth you aspire.

INQUIRY

To what state of being do I aspire?

PRACTICE

Notice your words and their impact. Get to know the one in you who is speaking them.

My words create positive effects
on those who hear them and
those about whom I speak.

REFLECTION

Imagine striking a beautiful bell. Masters who truly understood the nature of sound and form have crafted this bell with appreciation, love, respect, and listening. Imagine the sound of that resonating bell washing over and through you. Your heart opens, compelled by the beauty; your mind becomes peaceful and clear; your body relaxes in the sensual wash of the bell's tone. You are AWE Nature in resonance. Now imagine another bell that was created by someone in anger, judgment, criticism, blame and shame, doubt and fear. This bell is rigid, bent, jagged, distorted. Hit by the jarring sound, your heart closes, your mind becomes fragmented, and your body braces. Through words, you create either outcome.

INQUIRY

What bell will I choose to be?

PRACTICE

Today, speak only words that are resonant with your AWE Nature.

My words are not used as a weapon
against others or myself.

REFLECTION

It is so easy to lash out with words that hurt or diminish yourself or another. Ego gets caught in distorted reactions or defensive moves, aiming to hurt or be hurt. Words become weapons of destruction. You can learn to interrupt this reactive process, to intercept the impulse to speak hurtful words. If you are not willing, you are simply caught in fear. Distortion activates more distortion, and the cycle continues until you choose to release yourself. You can change the cycle in a defining moment. Will you react from fear or respond with words of love and appreciation?

INQUIRY

Is it time to forgive myself?

PRACTICE

Are you willing to stop using words as a weapon against yourself or others? Live one day at a time.

If you are not yet willing, then ask, What is needed for me to stop causing hurt?

I Am in a Good State of Words

My words evoke creativity, generosity, appreciation, and good action.

REFLECTION

Great leaders activate creativity. They understand that to spell a word is actually to cast a spell. The speaking of a word could either add to or negate the energy of what is taking place. Inherent in every moment is the possibility for anything—from the extraordinary to the mundane, kindness to meanness, joy to anger, life-giving energy to destruction. All is possible. Your words activate a creative force according to the intention that they carry. The mind hears and processes meaning, but the heart intuits the underlying intention of what is being spoken. Choose words that generate creativity, openness, beauty, generosity, and appreciation.

INQUIRY

How may I inspire creativity today?

PRACTICE

Engage this day with words of inspiration, creativity, appreciation, and good action.

Observe the result. Notice what shifts.

My words are carried by breath, which blows encouragement onto the embers of possibility for others and myself.

REFLECTION

A dream, a wish, a vision often begins as a tiny spark arising in consciousness. With no regard for convenience, the Universe calls you forth to service. It is now time for something beautiful to begin. This dream-fire pushes itself from the darkness below, seeking to fulfill its promise. Small and tender, it wants to become stronger. It will do just fine with the proper nurturing. While it is still young, supportive words carry oxygen to encourage it to reveal itself more and more. The embers of possibility beg to be nurtured by sweet words on your breath.

INQUIRY

What possibilities will I encourage today?

PRACTICE

Ask those you meet today about their dream.

Listen ever so deeply with encouragement.

I Am in a Good State of Words

My words are spoken cleanly in challenging situations, and I listen, listen, listen.

REFLECTION

Awkward and challenging situations will happen. We may experience misunderstandings, differences, debates, and conscious or unintentional meanness with others. When a comment hooks us, our distorted self engages, and we lash out with sarcasm, anger, or a hurtful reaction. How normal! If you are triggered, first take a breath, step back, and activate your AWE Nature with good intention. Be willing to risk messiness; address this event for the sake of getting to the other side. Now look into how you contributed to the situation. Listen, get curious, seek to understand what was going on for the other person involved. Express. Hold the good intention and speak your wisdom. Listen some more. Ask what the other person is hearing. Listen.

INQUIRY
What is my part in this?

PRACTICE
Breathe, listen, breathe, speak, breathe, listen.

I Am in a Good State of Words

My words give life to what desires to be born
and completion to what is ready to let go.

REFLECTION

Everything arises, passes through the cycle of life, and falls away, creating space for emergence. It is good to use our words to honor these cycles. In spring, we witness what is being born and give words to the dream that becomes our vision. In summer, we play as visionary words take form. Growth, structure, and development occur. In autumn, we acknowledge that endings are near. We speak our thanks and give appreciation. Letting go is at hand. In winter, the dream continues underground in dark shadows. On the surface, all seems at rest, yet the dream seed stirs relentlessly, calling us to respond.

I Am in a Good State of Words

INQUIRY

To what am I saying yes?
To what am I saying no?

PRACTICE

Notice what is arising and offer nurturing.

Notice what is continuing and offer energy.

Notice what is completing and let go.

My words are truthful, kind, and needed.

A traditional Sufi teaching asks us to consider our
  words before we speak.
There are three gates through which words must
  pass before being spoken.
The first gate asks, *"Are your words truthful?"*
  If they are not, they should not be spoken.
If they are, they then meet the second gate, which
  asks, *"Are your words kind?"*
If not, they should not be spoken.
If they are, they then pass to the third gate.
It asks, *"Are your words needed?"*
If they are, the words have passed through all
  three gates, and they may be spoken.

Are my words truthful, kind, and needed?

Use the three gates to assess your words. At
times it may result in less to say; at other
times, it may ask you to speak out more.

I Am in a Good State of Words

A Good State of Being

I am in a Good State of Being.

VERSE 38
I am Source and living as One with all.

VERSE 39
I am who I choose to be in this day's expression of the wholeness that I am.

VERSE 40
I regard all people, beings, and situations with the humility of one who meets a reflection of Universal beauty.

VERSE 41
Because I am in a Good State of Being, my spirit is bright and joyous.

VERSE 42
I am in right relationship with the Wisdom Field; therefore, I listen and respond according to the guidance of my AWE Nature.

VERSE 43
When I am experiencing discord with the wisdom of my AWE Nature, I look into the cause and ask what is needed. I then respond and follow through.

VERSE 44
Because I am in a Good State of Being, I am the source of my joy.

I Am in a Good State of Being

VERSE 45

I am in right relationship with my three wisdom portals—body, heart, and mind.

VERSE 46

I am in right relationship with my body; therefore, I treat my body with kindness, good food, exercise, and care.

VERSE 47

I am in right relationship with my heart and therefore check in often with my emotions. I activate my heart wisdom.

VERSE 48

I am in right relationship with my mind and therefore practice discernment of word and thought always.

VERSE 49

I love my shadow and the wholeness of my being.

VERSE 50

I am in right relationship with the earth and all beings, including the plants, animals, minerals, soil, waters, and every other aspect of earth and the surrounding Uni-verse.

VERSE 51

I am a beacon of light that shines loving-kindness for all, including myself.

VERSE 52

I live in trust of myself and therefore move forward in a good way.

VERSE 53

I am a lifelong learner. I allow myself to risk succeeding or failing and to learn always.

I am in a Good State of Being.

VERSE 38

I am Source and living as One with all.

REFLECTION

I died once, long ago. Whether by destiny or a fortunate accident, my body slumped to the floor. I was now observing the scene below. I experienced awareness of Light, Essence, Source. I was clearly not my body, which lay there lifeless; nor was I my thoughts or emotions. Awareness transcended form, space, and time. Presence, Expansiveness and Infinity abounded. Years later while meditating I slid onto the spiraling current deep within. I popped through and found Wisdom, Grace, and Love. Years later, I sat on a beach in India; I accidently slipped through a crack in time and again experienced Unity. The ocean stopped. Slumped, slid, slipped—all good accidents. I could list a thousand ideas about who we are not. There are no words for who we are. We are Source. Source is love. Source just is.

INQUIRY

Who am I really?

PRACTICE

Meditation is a great vehicle.
Find a local teacher.

VERSE 39

I am who I choose to be in this day's
expression of the wholeness that I am.

REFLECTION

In our human experience, we take on form, iden-
tity, meaning, and purpose. In Spirit, none of these
matter, but here we can choose who to be, what to
do, how to express our purpose, or not. You could
let the world design your life—be who you are hyp-
notized to be, do what is expected. For some, this
may be good wisdom, but others will be inspired
or called to a new adventure. To say yes will likely
disrupt one's safe, orderly life. Should you choose
to accept an invitation to a grand journey, begin
by opening to the emerging expression of you at
this time.

INQUIRY

Who is emerging from within?

PRACTICE

Create a collage of you according to your calling.

I regard all people, beings, and situations
with the humility of one who meets
a reflection of Universal beauty.

REFLECTION

This Universe is energy. The energy takes on form:
nuclear, atomic, cellular, material, mineral, plant,
insect, animal, fish, human, you.

Your awareness reflects the Universe in form; each
moment is its revelation. Remember to stay open,
to love and appreciate it all.

Avoid voting and judging what to like or not.

Allow yourself to be humbled by the beauty, to be
in awe, to be shattered by the experience of being
human. Celebrate your brilliant mind, emotional
experience, and sensuality of body.

With every thought, situation, and being you meet,
bow to your teacher.

INQUIRY

What is awe-full about this?

PRACTICE

When you turn away in judgment or fear, recover
with love and openness and ask what is needed.

VERSE 41

Because I am in a Good State of Being,
my spirit is bright and joyous.

REFLECTION

Just as the diamond cutter shapes and polishes a
rough stone to achieve its highest expression, we
too are cut, molded, and polished by life's challenges and opportunities. By choosing well and
learning how to engage experientially via our
AWE Nature, we access our highest possibility,
the essence of who we are. Indeed, we are bright
and joyous in spirit, which depends on no external
circumstance or condition.

INQUIRY

How will I meet the possibilities of this day?

PRACTICE

Notice a situation in your life that is distressful.

What is the gift of it? How can you
make friends with what is distressing?

Choose an action that will correct
the situation and follow through.

I am in right relationship with the Wisdom Field; therefore, I listen and respond according to the guidance of my AWE Nature.

REFLECTION

Ever wonder about the source of intuition? How can two people show up at the same time with the same breakthrough idea; or how can someone call just as you are thinking of him? These are examples of Wisdom Field experiences. When you are present to any one being, thing, or situation, there is a resonant field relationship between you. All beings contribute to the Universal Field. The earth, a forest, the ocean, a city, a team, an organization— all these have consciousness; a set of any two or more creates a field. If you attune to the wisdom in that field, you will find numerous insights.

INQUIRY

What is my hunch about a situation?

PRACTICE

Sit for 10 minutes in a quiet space. Open to a question regarding a situation you are involved in.

Allow any insight to occur through your mind, heart, or body. Notice; release it; listen some more.

VERSE 43

When I experience discord with the
wisdom of my AWE Nature, I look
into the cause and ask what is needed.
I then respond and follow through.

REFLECTION

AWE Nature is Awake, Wise, and Engaged. Awake
souls are grounded, clear, and free from distortion and illusion. Wise beings are able to access
information from the Wisdom Field beyond Self.
Engaged ones are open, flexible, and willing to
respond to life. Our hearts, minds, and bodies are
meant to harmonize like an orchestra. Resonance
occurs when you are in tune with your wisdom,
values, and purpose; dissonance arises when you
are out of touch or incongruent. Become still and
present, assess what is going on, and take courageous action as a regular practice.

INQUIRY

What is my intuition revealing at this time?

PRACTICE

Notice your level of resonance versus dissonance.

What courageous action have you been avoiding?

Because I am in a Good State of
Being, I am the source of my joy.

I Am in a Good State of Being

REFLECTION

I used to have a lot of stuff, and I made lots of money. Those were the good old days. I was happy, except when I wasn't. One day I awoke, walked away, and went on an adventure. All I had now was my backpack. Still, I was happy, except when I wasn't. One day, I awoke in a monastery and said yes to being a monk. Soon I had only four things: meditation beads, robes, razor, and a bowl. Still I was happy, except when I wasn't. One day as a monk, someone moved my bowl, my bowl, MY BOWL. A lightning bolt struck me down—I had identified my Self with a bowl. Freed from my bowl, there was only the Universe. Still I was happy, except when I wasn't. Now I have beautiful things again. Still I am happy, except when I'm not.

INQUIRY

What am I holding onto?

PRACTICE

Let go.

VERSE 45

*I am in right relationship with my three
wisdom portals—body, heart, and mind.*

REFLECTION

Wisdom is sourced from beyond your Self. We
access wisdom through heart, mind, and body
when we are open, present, and willing. There is no
age requirement for gaining wisdom. Both a child's
innocent observation and the timely pointing of
an elder show us the way to wisdom far beyond
intellect or past experience. Learn to access the
three portals of mind, body, and heart. You might
receive a blessing from the Wisdom Field as intuition (heart portal), a gut feeling (body portal), or
an insight (mind portal).

INQUIRY

What intuition is stirring my heart now?

What does my mind perceive right now?

What is my body sensing right now?

PRACTICE

Develop your capacity to access all
three portals through regular practice.

VERSE 46:

I am in right relationship with my
body; therefore, I treat my body with
kindness, good food, exercise, and care.

REFLECTION

Your body is the vehicle that carries you through
life. It offers direct experiences with the five sensu-
alities, plus movement and action. The body benefits from respect, care, good diet, and exercise. You
know this. Do your choices open the way to harm
or well-being? Do you understand how much a
healthful lifestyle will expand your AWE experiences? Your choices create karma. You will benefit
from paying attention to body signals and clues,
such as gut feelings, illness, and the stressing of
muscles. As a portal to the Wisdom Field, the body
senses beyond mind perception. It is always com-
municating with you.

INQUIRY

How will I show love and respect for my body?

PRACTICE

Choose one beneficial practice for your body and
form an accountability partnership with a friend.

I am in right relationship with my heart
and therefore check in often with my
emotions. I activate my heart wisdom.

REFLECTION

Your heart is the center for emotional experience and the insights of intuition. Awareness will
help you see that emotions exist as a response
to an event. Many people disconnect from emotions either by shutting down or exaggerating
their response. Learn to notice the early arising
of an emotion. Choose to engage in a good way
through your AWE Nature. It can be challenging
to discern if an emotional experience is yours or
someone else's. By grounding in AWE Nature, you
will experience balanced emotional responses to
life and know what is yours or not.

INQUIRY

What is activating my current emotions?

PRACTICE

Notice your emotional field as you tell the stories
of your day. Do you have a storytelling style
that recreates a certain emotional experience?

To what emotion may you be most addicted?

What does your storytelling habit get or cost you?

I Am in a Good State of Being

I am in right relationship with my mind
and therefore practice discernment
of word and thought always.

REFLECTION

The mind accesses the Wisdom Field by perceiving. In each second, it filters gigabits of information, allowing you to be aware of only as much as you can handle. When the mind perceives danger, it brings this to your attention. The problem is that the mind may imagine dangers where they don't really exist. Discerning mind instead ferrets out distortions, illusions, and lies. We connect to life through our stories. Distorted storyteller exaggerates or changes the story. AWE Nature tells stories in a good way. Experience peace by grounding in your AWE Nature, meditating, and creating beautiful, uncluttered surroundings.

INQUIRY

What is my present state of mind?

PRACTICE

Beauty profoundly affects your state of mind.
Raise the standard of beauty at home and work.

I love my shadow and the
wholeness of my being.

REFLECTION

Shadow is any aspect that operates beneath the surface. Secretly, you could be carrying hurt, anger, resentment, hunger for validation or belonging, and so on. We all know the shadow. If left unattended, this energy tends to leak out through hurtful behavior. Unconscious motives run like a script and lead to choices that block well-being. If you are getting angry for no reason, not liking people you don't even know, dropping good boundaries, repeating patterns of self-sabotage, being hurt repeatedly, or causing harm, then shadow is likely at play. Yet, you can incorporate its power and wisdom into your service in good ways, according to the wholeness of who you are.

INQUIRY

What am I continuously avoiding?

PRACTICE

Find a professional who has experience
working with shadow and go exploring.

I am in right relationship with earth and
all beings, including the plants, animals,
minerals, soil, waters, and every other aspect
of earth and the surrounding Uni-verse.

REFLECTION
Uni refers to One; *verse* means to turn toward.
Uni-verse is to turn toward the One. You are interrelated with everyone and everything in this
Uni-verse. You have direct impact in relationships
in which you are consciously aware, according to
the quality of your intentions, words, and actions.
You also are in relationship to all beings and aspects of the Uni-verse even when not consciously aware of them. In an awakened walk, you are
conscious of your effect on all beings, events, and
situations. You take responsibility for your part in
those relationships.

INQUIRY
How am I contributing in a good way?

PRACTICE
Identify a cause on earth that you care about.
You have an opportunity to contribute with your
thoughts, words, and actions. Follow through.

I Am in a Good State of Being

I am a beacon of light shining loving-
kindness for all, including myself.

REFLECTION

You communicate a lot through your body language, facial expressions, tone of voice, and changes of pace. The emotional field you are creating has an even greater power to affect others. When you enter a room, you are like a tincture that blends with the energy of the room. Walk through the room exuding anger or frustration and notice it spread to anyone who is susceptible in that moment. Or, walk through the same room emoting loving-kindness and be its source for those present. Be authentic about your feelings. If you feel frustration, experience it fully and then allow it to pass. If you are attached to a certain emotion and don't want it to pass, you may be in distortion.

INQUIRY

Today I will be a beacon of what state?

PRACTICE

Choose an impact you would like to have on the people you meet today (e.g., happy, frustrated, inspired, beaten). Now bring that with you.

I Am in a Good State of Being

I live in trust of myself and therefore
move forward in a good way.

REFLECTION

Trust must begin with Self. Do not give your power away to another just because you do not trust yourself. For what can you trust yourself? To never make a mistake? Only by playing small. To not sound or look foolish? Only if you don't speak out. Can you trust yourself to never fall? Only if you don't get up in the first place. So what can you trust self for? To learn, to grow, to get up, to try again, to laugh, to take risks, to stretch, to dream, to be beautiful, to recover, to love.

INQUIRY

What is possible when I fully trust in myself?

PRACTICE

Notice where you are playing safe or avoiding your call. Ask, "Am I now ready for that risk?"

Access your wisdom and choose a courageous action to move that part of your life forward.

Follow through.

VERSE 53

I am a lifelong learner. I allow myself to risk
succeeding or failing and to learn always.

REFLECTION

The one thing on which we can count is that life
will continually challenge us; therefore, learning
is a lifelong prospect. When you meet life's risks,
having a good attitude toward learning supports
you. Many of the greatest experiences one encoun-
ters are risky: saying yes or no to relationships, job
opportunities, and entrepreneurial callings; being an artist or public speaker; raising a family or
investing in a dream. We will never be able to plan
our way around risk or control circumstances to
avoid it. All we can do, all we need to do, is move
courageously, wisely, and willingly. We will win
some and lose some, yet we will always learn.

INQUIRY
What is life calling me to?

PRACTICE
Attend to what stirs your heart
and mind at this time?

What will you say yes to?
Or no to?

A Good State of Purpose

I am in a Good State of Purpose.

VERSE 54

I am beyond the box that would allow only one stated purpose. I willingly commit to my highest expression of purpose each day.

VERSE 55

I embrace the gift of this precious life and the opportunity to be—sensually, emotionally, and mindfully—all that is in accordance with my AWE Wisdom.

VERSE 56

I am well used as I stay present to my experience.

VERSE 57

I am not attached to any particular direction on my path; therefore, I am available to my vision, my purpose, and the dream Universe.

VERSE 58

I honor the gift of this life, and I unfold my purpose daily according to my AWE Nature.

VERSE 59

I understand that the ultimate purpose of this precious life is a great mystery.

VERSE 60

I author my moment-by-moment unfolding as I dance with the emerging story of the Universe.

VERSE 61

I allow my purpose to emerge from each Now moment; therefore, I remain open to the call of my AWE Nature and the Universe.

VERSE 62

According to my wisdom, I live beyond unconscious, limiting expectations and willingly take risks to expand myself and the well-being of All.

VERSE 63

Our purposes are interrelated; therefore, I am available to support you and others as we fulfill life's call.

VERSE 64

I am in a Good State of Purpose; therefore, my livelihood honors the values of my AWE Nature.

VERSE 65

My success is not measured by the size or results of my efforts but by the beauty that comes from how I respond in each passing moment.

VERSE 66

I unfold my purpose simply through each breath and sweep of the broom.

VERSE 67

In each moment, I am in-joy and on purpose in a good way.

I am in a Good State of Purpose.

I am beyond the box that would allow only one stated purpose. I willingly commit to my highest expression of purpose each day.

REFLECTION

Give your Self over to today's expression of purpose as inspired by your wisdom. Your consciousness is capable of infinite expansion. Learn to open—mind, heart, and body—to AWE Nature with the realization of your kinship to All. Use the expansiveness of heart to focus and direct energy like light through a magnifying lens. It will travel toward any intention that is informed by your wisdom. May simple laughter, play, and joy be the ultimate expression of your life today.

INQUIRY

How may I express my joy today?

PRACTICE

If you are called to take on a project for the sake of something beyond, then act now in a good way.

If you have no particular project
tickling your feet into action, then
play like the blessed child you are.

(sidebar) I Am in a Good State of Purpose

I embrace the gift of this precious life
and the opportunity to be—sensually,
emotionally, and mindfully—all that is
in accordance with my AWE Wisdom.

REFLECTION

What other reason for life if not to live it fully? Consider the gifts we humans carry that distinguish us from most other beings on earth. Through mind, we have the capacity for great creativity, insight, and communication. Through heart, we may connect, emote, and motivate courageously. Embodied, we can experience heightened senses via sight, sound, touch, taste, and smell. We can know deep suffering or great joy. The teacher Buddha experimented with both ascetics and hedonism. Neither prescription supported his awakening. He took instead a middle path and gained infinite wisdom.

INQUIRY

What is amazing about this day?

PRACTICE

Give yourself the presence of a five-sense day.

I Am in a Good State of Purpose

I am well used as I stay present to my experience.

REFLECTION

There are many jobs that keep society functioning. In the middle of the night, a street is washed, garbage is collected, a police officer watches, a firefighter stands by ready to rush into danger. All day long, teachers work with learners, taxi drivers move us around, salespeople connect with solutions, administrators keep things running, interior designers make it beautiful, gardeners keep it alive, programmers create code, dreamers dream, and parents raise children as best they can. We all have the opportunity to bring heart, mind, and body to the experience. Show up with the greatness and wholeness of who you are.

INQUIRY

What is meaningful about the job I do today?

PRACTICE

Journal about how the job you are doing today meets your personal talent and genius.

If you want to expand your career, then do at least one thing today to create that opportunity.

I Am in a Good State of Purpose

I am not attached to any particular direction on my path; therefore, I am available to my vision, my purpose, and the dream Universe.

REFLECTION

Once upon a time, I had a great business, a great life, friends, and lovers. One morning, I awoke to a familiar stirring deep within (from where I cannot say exactly, just as I cannot say where my soul resides). Inspiration was dawning! My heart beat strongly, guiding me toward some purpose. Deep within, I knew a great flight was in the wings. I looked eastward out the window. Feeling the breeze on my face, I promised to follow the wind and my wisdom. With no plan and a one-way plane ticket, I responded to the Uni-verse. My family and friends were mystified. "I'll be back in a month or so," I offered to quiet them and myself. Almost two years later, I returned. Oh, what an adventure! In retrospect I couldn't have known beforehand what to ask for. Just say yes, and allow the mystery to reveal its dream to you.

INQUIRY
What is calling?

PRACTICE
When you are called, answer!

VERSE 58

I honor the gift of this life, and I unfold my
purpose daily according to my AWE Nature.

REFLECTION

Life is a precious gift filled with wonder, possibility, love, play, and much to do. However, in picking at imperfections, we miss what is suitable. In
resisting the tide, we confound its lift. In grasping
for more, we forget to receive. In being indepen-
dent, we shut others out. In feeling fear, we cut off
love. In holding doubt, we reject our amazing Self.
With no handy instructions for which way is best,
we are left to our own devices. Thankfully, we have
great minds for perceiving what is, open hearts for
feeling what could be, and strong bodies to take us
quickly there.

INQUIRY

What is my purpose today?

PRACTICE

Take a walk through a crowded place
today. As you stride with appreciation
for All, be prepared to stay open and
respond to the possibilities in each step.

I Am in a Good State of Purpose

I understand that the ultimate purpose
of this precious life is a great mystery.

REFLECTION

I died once. I came back with a direct experience
with the Divine, which I cannot fully explain. A
loved one died once. His spirit appeared before
me, and I spoke with him. He moved on, which I
cannot fully explain. A frightened man put a gun
to my head once and said he would shoot me. He
didn't, which I cannot fully explain. I was desper-
ate for help once. I was lost and didn't know what
to do. The phone rang with the answer, which I
cannot fully explain. I was driving on an icy road
once. Six children leapt directly in front of my
skidding car. I could not stop. A voice said, "Do not
sound the horn." I slid silently between their innocent faces. I cannot fully explain that.

INQUIRY

How available am I to play in the mystery?

PRACTICE

Notice the mysteries of your own life.

VERSE 60

I author my moment-by-moment unfolding as I
dance with the emerging story of the Universe.

REFLECTION

Children dance in the wonder of play and discovery. You create, then move on to create again. Your
life is a canvas, reflecting Inspiration as embodied spirit. You spiral and twirl, while life mirrors
your fluid heart. If you become rigid, well, that is
still a dance. Something must give eventually. Even
within the structure of an established life, there's
full opportunity to be the magician. This Universe
is unfolding its present story. What a privilege to
witness and in-joy such a great adventure. As the
author of your life, choose how to respond as the
dance floor shifts around you.

INQUIRY

What story will I dance today?

PRACTICE

As you are the author of this life, the Universe
is your lover. Write a story, draw a picture, or
create a dance that illustrates your love affair.

I Am in a Good State of Purpose

I allow my purpose to emerge from each Now
moment; therefore, I remain open to the
call of my AWE Nature and the Universe.

REFLECTION

We change over time; we learn, mature, and
develop. The world also changes. Kids grow up,
industries come and go, yesterday's hot spot is today's old news. In the current quickening, more
than ever we will witness shifts in the world. Your
AWE Nature is always curious and available to respond according to what is wanted now . . . and
then now . . . and again now. Every wave has three
phases—the leading edge, the middle, and the end.
Each phase is awash with opportunity. It is helpful to know the phase of your wave as you keep life
flowing. By staying awake, wise, and engaged, you
will always be relevant. Find a special way to engage
or be of service and thus fulfill your purpose.

INQUIRY

What is being asked of me? Where am I resisting?

PRACTICE

What is the best use of your genius now?

I Am in a Good State of Purpose

According to my wisdom, I live beyond
unconscious, limiting expectations
and willingly take risks to expand
myself and the well-being of All.

REFLECTION

There is tension in life between conforming and
being a maverick. The choice is yours to make
when you are conscious, aware of the big picture,
courageous, and connected to AWE Nature, your
source of inspiration. What might be the highest
and best service? Wisdom is key here. Neither con-
formists nor mavericks are inherently good or bad.
Rebelling just for the sake of disruption is being
a slave to rebellion. Conforming without question
is abandoning creative spirit. Every great transformation meets resistance in the status quo. Every
living system has a raison d'être.

INQUIRY

As courage meets inspiration, what will I do?

PRACTICE

Get to know the one in you who conforms
and the one who is a maverick.

Our purposes are interrelated; therefore,
I am available to support you and
others as we fulfill life's call.

REFLECTION

There was a time when victory at any cost was
revered. In that era, slavery was accepted and
profit ruled the moral compass.

Later, belonging was expected and communality
seemed the way. All for one and one for all; stay
in line and don't poke your head up.

Then initiative reemerged and the iconic leader
ruled again. Competition, climbing over backs,
and quarterly profits governed the day.

Inspired by the Wisdom Field, we are now ready
for all to benefit—creativity, genius, prosperity,
seven-generation thinking, cooperation, leadership, joining, and emerging are forthcoming.
Love will prevail as we are flexible and respond
according to our AWE Nature.

INQUIRY

Who is receptive to my support today?

PRACTICE

Give; receive; follow; lead; listen; love.

I Am in a Good State of Purpose

I am in a Good State of Purpose; therefore, my livelihood honors the values of my AWE Nature.

REFLECTION

Not all jobs, businesses, and paths are suited to all people. Are your values aligned with the contribution of your walk in the world? Your AWE Nature will resonate with activity most aligned to your personal genius, talents, values, and purpose. It's one thing to do a job about which you are not excited; it's something else altogether to do work that goes against your values. It takes courage to make bold moves, but what is life if not to be well used? Blessings be on those who serve this amazing Universe and remain joyfully congruent with their purpose.

INQUIRY

How could my livelihood more suitably honor my value system?

PRACTICE

List what is important according to your vision, dreams, and purpose.

Notice if there are any gaps.

Lead your career and life's purpose into greater alignment.

VERSE 65

My success is not measured by the size or results
of my efforts but by the beauty that comes
from how I respond in each passing moment.

REFLECTION

We may live into meaning and purpose with complex, entangled projects or in the simplest of ways. To enjoy success, walk through this day sending appreciation and encouragement to everyone you pass by, or join a team that is raising awareness about the distress of the world's oceans, or build better communities to uplift the future of our children. You are influencing your world through every thought, word, and action. Consider this: Through my thought, word, or action, am I creating beauty? Am I providing life-giving energy? If so, then you are well on the path of living into your highest purpose.

INQUIRY

What is the nature of my impact in the world?

PRACTICE

Create the intention to generate a wake of beauty and provide life-giving energy to those who cross your path today.

I unfold my purpose simply through
each breath and sweep of the broom.

REFLECTION

When I was a Buddhist monk in Burma (Myanmar), I lived at beautiful monastery once surrounded by the jungle, but now by the city. Old trees lined the pathways and constantly shed an abundance of leaves, twigs, and mangos. Every day I wandered through the grounds in awe of the beauty. One day, my attention followed a forgotten pathway buried knee deep in musty leaves. The path inspired me to reclaim it, so I began. The enormity of this task was soon apparent. The work was intense, and my distortions said it was too hot, too much, and not worth the effort. Still, I heard the call. Before long, several monks joined me, and then several people came from the nearby village. Their faces glowed. Together we claimed our emerging path.

INQUIRY

What path is calling me?

PRACTICE

Just start sweeping.

In each moment, I am in-joy and
on purpose in a good way.

REFLECTION

Joy is the essence of your being. It is in the moment
as you turn to the Oneness. It is incompatible, however, with the illusions of ego. When you surrender
the mistaken concepts of separation, gratifica-
tion, material happiness, or conditional love, joy
appears. It descends when you are shattered by the
beauty and simplicity of life. If deep suffering hob-
bles your efforts, exhausted, you finally fall into
joy. Joy was there all along, except you couldn't see
it, feel it, or know it—until you were at last open
enough to give up being alone, busy, grasping,
avoiding, or chasing. Once opened, in awareness,
you will not be lost. You are Joy. Joy just is.

INQUIRY

How am I joy?

PRACTICE

Move through a crowded market and leave a sense
of lift under the wings of everyone you meet.

I Am in a Good State of Purpose

A Good State of Effort

I am in a Good State of Effort.

VERSE 68

I apply good effort each day to allow my call to be expressed according to the inspiration received through wisdom.

VERSE 69

Because I am in a Good State of Effort, I am mindful in each moment.

VERSE 70

I hold effort and mindfulness with commitment, beauty, ease, delight, and flow.

VERSE 71

As I am at choice, I apply my will to follow through and move forward according to my choice.

VERSE 72

My problems are just challenges that invite me to engage in a good way.

VERSE 73

I am flexible, allowing my emotions, stories, and beliefs to shift in accordance with my growth and the wisdom of my AWE Nature.

VERSE 74

When I want someone or something around me to be different, I apply the right measure of effort to be responsible and to become that myself first.

VERSE 75

I apply good effort to remember my genius, talents,

and gifts and to be mindful of the stories I repeat about myself.

I attend to what is needed with wisdom rather than aversion, attraction, or attachment.

VERSE 77
I apply the right measure of energy to follow through and complete what I intend—with ease, delight, and respect for cycles and timing. I apply my will in a good way.

VERSE 78
I apply the effort of appreciation for every being and situation I have attracted to my life. Releasing judgment, I apply good effort to recover to openness, listening, curiosity, and understanding.

VERSE 79
I am actively compassionate and forgiving to all, including myself.

VERSE 80
I honor cycles and timing, remaining at choice about when to act and when to be still.

VERSE 81
I look into each moment and ask what is needed. I respond with the wisdom of my AWE Nature.

VERSE 82
I accept that life will have many beginnings and endings, successes and failings. Every day is a good day to begin again.

I am in a Good State of Effort.

I Am in a Good State of Effort

VERSE 68

I apply good effort each day to allow
my call to be expressed according to the
inspiration received through wisdom.

REFLECTION

Compassionate effort is useful to sustain your
AWE Nature and to express your Self each day.
This effort could be similar to that of turning with
pleasure to the warm sun on a gently lit day. Or, it
might be more like what is needed to step across a
stream, directing your feet to land atop wet irregular
stones. It could be like the effort of catching
yourself when you have slipped on an icy walkway.
It could be the effort of determination to get
to the top of a vertical mountain path. It could be
the effort needed when your life has been uprooted
from losing a job. It could be what is needed
after losing a loved one and the kids need to be fed.
It could be the effort of staying in love effortlessly.

INQUIRY

What effort is my wisdom expressing now?

PRACTICE

Apply good effort to be awake, wise, and engaged.

Because I am in a Good State of Effort,
I am mindful in each moment.

REFLECTION

Mindfulness is simply being present to what is. Be present to your emotions, physical surroundings, and thoughts, and those you are with. You can even daydream and be present to the fact that you are daydreaming. You may focus on a task or mindfully create a space in which you may wonder about what might be. You have the capacity to observe if you have become caught in your distorted self. With good effort, you may choose to recover easily and delightfully to your AWE Nature. Practice and develop a reliable Observer that will provide reports to you regarding your overall state—through your body, mind, and emotional experiences. Observe lightly with joy and ease.

INQUIRY

What is my Observer noticing right now?

PRACTICE

Check in with your Observer before, during, and after events of this day. Remember also to check in with your mind, body, and heart wisdom.

I Am in a Good State of Effort

VERSE 70

I hold effort and mindfulness with
commitment, beauty, ease, delight, and flow.

REFLECTION

The beauty of effort is being in flow, in the ease of synchronicity. You soon reach a zone of delightful performance, where mind is behind and body and heart are in front. You feel commitment to the experience and trust in the natural, perfect approach toward each turn in the road. In the moment-by-moment rhythm of creating your inspiration, you soar. Motor biking calls for a relationship between the rider, the motorcycle, and the road. You engage in a dance of weaving through high-speed corners, eyes setting turn-in points, ears tuned to optimizing shifts, body sensing the grip of the rubber as you lean courageously into each corner. Trusting and committed, you feel it all come together.

INQUIRY
In what way might I be trying too hard?

PRACTICE
Notice the degree of flow in your movements.

Where can you lean in more?
Or let go?

I Am in a Good State of Effort

As I am at choice, I apply my
will to follow through and move
forward according to my choice.

REFLECTION

Moving through life in a good way is a process of intention, choice, good action, and follow through with responsibility for the outcome. You must be willing to take responsibility for your life. Start by activating your AWE Nature. Now it is time to make a good choice. To do that, you must be willing to create a variety of options. Otherwise, you would not really be choosing, but just pretending. Create at least three possibilities of response to any life situation. Using the wisdom of your AWE Nature, you will make a great choice. Next, activate your will to follow through. This is a good application of will power.

INQUIRY

What are three choices so that I may move
forward in action in a good way?

PRACTICE

Choose a situation that you are in. Apply the process just described and notice the result.

VERSE 72

My problems are just challenges that
invite me to engage in a good way.

REFLECTION

What is the difference between a problem or
obstacle and an opportunity? Absolutely nothing
until the moment you label it. Then it becomes
whatever you have named it. You will meet this
event according to how you choose to show up
for it. The Universe has no opinion of problems,
challenges, or opportunities. The Universe has no
opinion of you. There is nothing personal in any of
it until you make it so. Regardless of how you view
the events of your life, you always get to choose
how to engage. Choose your way of intending and
engaging.

INQUIRY

What is the nature of the situation I meet today?

PRACTICE

Choose resourceful views
for what you meet today.

I Am in a Good State of Effort

110 / I AM IN A GOOD STATE OF EFFORT

I am flexible, allowing my emotions, stories, and beliefs to shift in accordance with my growth and the wisdom of my AWE Nature.

REFLECTION

Through AWE Nature we are flexible. Emotions move through us; the stories we tell of experiences shift as we heal and develop our relationship to an event. Beliefs are informed by our own wisdom. As we experience new insight, we are willing to shift to a more current understanding, one that is congruent with expanded consciousness. Distorted self tends to lock onto or avoid emotional states, is unwilling to shift, and recreates stories about daily and life experiences that drive a mistaken agenda, such as suffering or wrongness. Notice and be present to your current state of being. Perhaps you are carrying some story that you can put down. Only you can know.

INQUIRY

What is it time for me to set down?

PRACTICE

Be fully present to a recent or past life event, your story of it, your emotional experience. Allow a shift.

I Am in a Good State of Effort

When I want someone or something around me
to be different, I apply the right measure of effort
to be responsible and to become that myself first.

REFLECTION

Ever been in situations with other people and wanted them or the situation to be different? It seldom
works out to just wish or demand change. We have
contributed to how others around us are behaving. You may be thinking, "It is not me; they are the
ones behaving poorly." This is a "yes . . . and" situation. They may be behaving poorly and you have
also contributed to the relationship. First, check in
with your Self and ask, "How am I contributing to
this situation?" Adjust from your side first. If you
want respect, respect yourself first. For kindness,
be kind. For generosity, be generous. Maintain
good boundaries and honor your well-being! We
are mirrors for each other.

INQUIRY
What is the mirror of life reflecting to me?

PRACTICE
Practice being self-responsible for your life.

I apply good effort to remember my
genius, talents, and gifts and to be mindful
of the stories I repeat about myself.

REFLECTION

Through AWE Nature you are easily connected to your genius, talents, and gifts. By applying good effort, you are able to bring these qualities to everything you do. Life is then play, work, service, and a beautiful expression of the unique bundle that you are. This includes being honest, humble, and authentic through the stories you tell yourself and others about your life and adventures. Tell stories that reflect your beauty, genius, and triumph. Coming from AWE Nature, these stories carry hope, inspiration, healing, and wisdom to uplift the world. Celebrate also your ups and downs, mistakes and learning, folly and brilliance.

INQUIRY
What are my gifts? What is my genius?

PRACTICE
Engage through your genius.

I Am in a Good State of Effort

VERSE 76

I attend to what is needed with wisdom rather than aversion, attraction, or attachment.

REFLECTION

In AWE Nature, I am connected to wisdom and choose what is needed. In distortion, however, I avoid. Even though some avoiding may be helpful, such as avoiding the pain of missed appointments, this is not informed by wisdom. In distortion, I am attracted. Even though attraction can be helpful, such as striving for goals, the energy of attraction is not of wisdom. In distortion, I am attached. Even though being attached to good things seems okay, the energy of attachment is not of wisdom. Through my AWE Nature, I am at choice about when to say yes or no. I choose flexibility in every aspect of my path and am therefore available to choose in a good way.

INQUIRY
What do I need for wisdom?

PRACTICE
Notice how you move and motivate yourself.

I apply the right measure of energy to follow through and complete what I intend—with ease, delight, and respect for cycles and timing. I apply my will in a good way.

REFLECTION

When you want to get going, it is time to activate your will with good effort. Do you ever approach the trailhead and turn back because it looks more difficult than you thought? When success looms, the status quo gets resistant, and you may hear the voice of quitting. Energies of doubt, procrastination, and fear may well up. "Not today; leave good enough alone," the voice pleads. Do not go to sleep. There is everything to lose as far as that dream is concerned. Activate your will and move through resistance with ease, delight, and respect for the cycle and timing of your great adventure. Take the first step, then the second, the third . . .

INQUIRY
Am I choosing the dream or the sleep?

PRACTICE
Activate your will and move in a good way.

I apply the effort of appreciation for
every being and situation I have attracted
to my life. Releasing judgment, I apply
good effort and recover to openness,
listening, curiosity, and understanding.

REFLECTION

For what are you grateful? Or not? All that is in your life reflects your ability to create. Even when things seem wrong or inconvenient, they carry a teaching. Before rushing to change anything, appreciate it first. Consider what learning the person or situation has brought. When you perceive something to be good, this is easy. For what you perceive undesirable, such as the influence of what didn't work out or situations you think went against you, the task is more challenging . . . and more important. Appreciate first, look for the teaching, choose what needs to happen, and follow through.

INQUIRY

What do I appreciate about my challenges in life?

PRACTICE

Journal appreciation for some person,
thing, or situation. It is here to teach you.

What did it bring?

What is beautiful?

What are you learning?

I am actively compassionate and
forgiving to all, including myself.

REFLECTION

People and events can cause us hurt, suffering, or loss. These moments happen in everyone's life. Afterward, it is in your hands and heart how to respond. If you attach yourself to the wound, you will keep repeating the hurt. You could blame or judge yourself or another. Or, you could respond from AWE Nature. Activate an Observer's report on what happened. Be present to your emotional, mental, and physical experience. Allow the time needed for healing. Be willing to move forward in a good way. Look into how you contributed to this situation. You will be more available to heal, learn, and grow. Take care of yourself, which may involve holding someone else accountable for his or her action. Do so with compassion because we are all humans on our human journey.

INQUIRY
Where can I apply compassion today?

PRACTICE
Assess what is needed through compassion?

I Am in a Good State of Effort

VERSE 80

I honor cycles and timing, remaining at choice
about when to act and when to be still.

REFLECTION

Some folks are like bulls, charging forward over
anything that gets in the way. They get a job done.
They get results, but often at the expense of those
who were run over by the charge. Others are more
like moss, lying low, waiting and waiting, easy
to walk on, pretty to look at. Yet, even moss gets
results. It benefits us to learn how to break free
from every habit—be it bull, moss, or anything
in-between. Learn to engage the moment and
situation you are in with a good measure of effort
and with respect for the cycle and timing of your
idea or project. Choose what response is wanted at
this time according to your highest wisdom.

INQUIRY
What is wanted from me now?

PRACTICE
By realizing whether you are responding
to life through habit or by choosing a good
response, you will be able to navigate a wise
course in accordance with your own wisdom.

I Am in a Good State of Effort

I look into each moment and ask what is needed.
I respond with the wisdom of my AWE Nature.

REFLECTION

Walking with curiosity is far more powerful than grasping for an answer. Our very culture pressures us to have answers, plans, solutions. But I have never seen a plan smart enough to predict every future; nor an answer that could represent all possibilities; nor only one right way to move. It takes courage to stay open, flexible, and present to new choices. There is much power in simple questions. Activate listening and curiosity and be willing to hear. Ask with an open hand, mind, and heart and consider any wisdom that comes through.

INQUIRY

What is trying to happen?

PRACTICE

Notice a situation in which you are sure you are right in your course of action. Reopen to new possibilities by asking some simple questions.

I Am in a Good State of Effort

I accept that life will have many beginnings and endings, successes and failings. Every day is a good day to begin again.

REFLECTION

In every ending, there is a new beginning, and after every setback, advancement. You grow and change, and the world changes around you. When something fails, begin again. When you overstay your welcome and your service is no longer needed where you are, then begin again. Recognize the timing and embrace the opportunity to reinvent yourself, or the world will send a memo of release in some other way. Though this may upset the quiet and order of your life, or even trigger a time of hardship, it is also an invitation to realign your genius with what the world needs now. This is where flexibility really serves. You will find new relevance and a call to attend the amazing game of life if you are willing to be flexible and begin again.

INQUIRY
What opportunity sparkles for me now?

PRACTICE
Follow your hunch about what is calling.

I Am in a Good State of Effort

A Good State of Practice
I am in a Good State of Practice.

VERSE 83

I practice and develop the art of expressing my being, values, and purpose daily.

VERSE 84

Each day I check in with my inner and outer experience, my state of being.

VERSE 85

I create my day consciously and care for my state of being.

VERSE 86

I plan my day according to AWE Nature's wisdom. I am intentional and flexible as the mystery in each moment unfolds.

VERSE 87

I care daily for my physical body, mind, emotional body, and spirit.

VERSE 88

In each day, I have a time of stillness. I listen to the beating of my heart, to my breath, and to the call of the Universe.

VERSE 89

Each day I meditate.

VERSE 90

I consciously express love and appreciate all that shows up in the unfolding of my journey, including the things that seem unpleasant or inconvenient.

VERSE 91

I check in with the Wisdom Field each day and ask what is needed. I listen and respond according to my AWE Nature.

VERSE 92

Each day I create internal beauty; I breathe in love. I create beauty and order in the space around me; I breathe out love and send life-giving energy to all beings.

VERSE 93

I notice what I repeatedly experience and project, such as fear, judgment, appreciation, being stuck, anger, or frenzy. I examine my contribution to each experience, which reveals what is in shadow.

VERSE 94

Each day I take a risk, a good action that is informed by my AWE Nature. I notice the cycle and timing of events and initiate what is ripe for beginning, nurture what is continuing, and bring completion to each ending.

VERSE 95

Each day I play, I laugh, I cry as a good response to what is unfolding around me.

VERSE 96

I keep the agreements I make with others and myself.

VERSE 97

I care for my relationships. Each day I reach out and add value to the life of another.

I am in a Good State of Practice.

I practice and develop the art of expressing
my being, values, and purpose daily.

REFLECTION

When I enter an unfamiliar industry, I first assess
who I need to be for the sake of excellence in that
role. For example, if I am president of a new com-
pany, I claim and become that now, present tense,
in the being and the doing. I get clear about what
I am great at, or just good at. I also discover what
skills and strengths I need to develop. I then set
about developing myself to be excellent in that
opportunity. I practice, practice, practice. Regardless of the title, job, or business you undertake,
always be congruent with your values. By staying
true to who you are and following your wisdom,
you will be met by people and opportunities as one
who is authentic. Authenticity is the single greatest
quality of leadership.

INQUIRY

What could I practice for the sake of excellence?

PRACTICE

Identify your gifts and gaps and then practice.

I Am in a Good State of Practice

Each day I check in with my inner and
outer experience, my state of being.

REFLECTION

I love those signs in the parks that say, "You are here!"
They always seem to be right. To get to where you
are going, it helps to know where and how you are
now. First, you can activate an Observer memo for
your current status, both internally and externally.
What is your overall state of well-being? Take stock
of your resources, the condition of your team, the
project, and the world in which you are operating.
Then reassess your plan or strategy; gather and as-
semble the resources needed for your project. If
you observe that your team is tired or stressed, you
might consider a day of play. If frenzy prevails, lead
a session of deep breathing and walk in a nearby
park. It is important to be aware.

INQUIRY

What is my present condition?

PRACTICE

Create a daily practice of checking
in and calibrating as needed.

I Am in a Good State of Practice

VERSE 85

I create my day consciously and
care for my state of being.

REFLECTION

Be effective through grounding, presence, and in-tention. It begins with choosing how you want to engage in each moment. If action is needed, use the in-tension of good commitment regarding goals and actions. By taking a step at a time, do at least one thing to move your agenda forward with great results. Some days or weeks require longer stretches of focus and effort; other times flow more easily. Balance focused activity with being out of space-time—dream, float, or move on the wind with no particular place to go. Allow heart, mind, and body to decompress and invite your inner child for a day of play. There are great things in the making.

INQUIRY

Work or play? What will I create this day?

PRACTICE

Each day do at least one thing to move
your plan forward, one thing to care for
yourself, and one thing to support another.

I plan my day according to AWE Nature's wisdom. I am intentional and flexible as the mystery in each moment unfolds.

REFLECTION

To plan is to put thought, intention, and purpose into locating needed resources and creating an effective strategy. Yet, as the expression goes, God laughs while humans make their plans. The strongest, most sustainable and durable elements of this world therefore are flexible. Trees survive storms because they bend; tall buildings and bridges survive nature's forces because they move. When things are no longer flexible, they are likely to break down and die. We engage each day with good intentions, plans, ideas, hopes, dreams, and concerns. Regardless of what plans we hold as the day begins, there is always time to dance and shift according to the ever-changing direction of the wind.

INQUIRY

What is needed today, will-power or flex-ability?

PRACTICE

Rather than try harder, try something else.

I Am in a Good State of Practice

VERSE 87

I care daily for my physical body,
mind, emotional body, and spirit.

REFLECTION

Each personal portal to wisdom (mind, body, and
heart) has both a biological aspect and a realm of
wisdom it can easily access. At the mind portal,
the brain governs the realm of thinking, assessing,
choosing, and the wisdom of perceiving. Through
the body we connect physically with sensing, action, movement, structure, and the wisdom of
gut feelings. Through the heart, we literally have
a beating heart and breathing lungs and access
the emotional, connecting, relational, intuitive
realm. Through the heart, we also experience interrelatedness. In creating practices that address
the wellness of your whole being, remember to
consider all three portals of wisdom—literally
and metaphorically.

INQUIRY

Which wisdom portal will I explore today?

PRACTICE

Consider mind, body, and heart when choosing
daily practices. Be sure to address all three.

I Am in a Good State of Practice

In each day, I have a time of stillness. I listen to the beating of my heart, to my breath, and to the call of the Universe.

REFLECTION

There are few other practices as universally beneficial as the daily practice of stillness. This is a time to step aside from the busyness, from the treadmill, from routines. You might stroll through a park or sit in a garden and enjoy tea, just taking in the beauty of what is. This is not the time for lists, emails, texting, or even meditation. Of course, meditation is another great practice, but not a substitute for stillness. Allow your thoughts to become quiet. As sights and sounds pass through you, allow your heart to beat easily. Allow your breath to be deep and full. Allow your body to relax. Allow the beauty of the moment to move you as Self falls into stillness. Allow the world to carry on.

INQUIRY

What is being revealed through stillness today?

PRACTICE

Allow.

I Am in a Good State of Practice

Each day I meditate.

REFLECTION

Meditation is a valuable daily practice. Its benefits include energizing and clarifying the mind, calming the heart, and allowing you to notice the present condition of the body. There are many kinds of meditation. Some are more active, such as forms of yoga or walking meditation. Some are more physically still, such as sitting meditation. Some follow mantras, while others follow the breath. All styles and methods are beneficial, and the results may vary. In all cases, it is helpful to have the guidance of an experienced teacher. A guide can shape your technique and also support you because meditation often stirs up energies that have been previously lying dormant.

INQUIRY

What do I make more important than well-being?

PRACTICE

Meditate twice today, whether for 1 or 15 minutes.

I Am in a Good State of Practice

VERSE 90

I consciously express love and appreciate
all that shows up in the unfolding of
my journey, including the things that
seem unpleasant or inconvenient.

REFLECTION

It is easy to appreciate what you like. The real challenge is to value what you do not necessarily welcome or agree with. Everything brings opportunities for learning, strengthening, or shifting in some way. By meeting life with appreciation, you open to grow and create from all. Through curiosity and listening, you gain respect and a new view of life. When you lead with love, appreciation, and respect, the world will find that in you. Judgment brings more separation; appreciation leads to Oneness.

INQUIRY

As I face into what seems inconvenient,
what can I appreciate?

PRACTICE

With every person or situation, find what you can truly appreciate and respect. Always be authentic.

VERSE 91

I check in with the Wisdom Field each
day and ask what is needed. I listen and
respond according to my AWE Nature.

REFLECTION

There is a collective consciousness, a unity of
wisdom to which we each contribute and may
draw from at all times. All you need do is to open
the wisdom portals of heart, mind, and body. Then
tune in while letting go of what you already know.
With each passing day, conditions in the world will
require a different response than you could have
previously known or foreseen. Your knowledge
and history provide only adequate ideas, not ones
that are inspired and brilliant or that could radi-
cally reshape your path. Look into the world's subtle space, into the Wisdom Field, for intuition, insight, inspiration. Then take on the risk and act for
the sake of something greater than yourself. This
you must do each day.

INQUIRY

What is my wisdom today?

PRACTICE

Choose to live according to your in-spire-ation.

I Am in a Good State of Practice

VERSE 92

Each day I create internal beauty; I breathe
in love. I create beauty and order in the
space around me; I breathe out love and
send life-giving energy to all beings.

REFLECTION

Create your life experience from the center out.
Breathe into your center; imagine breathing in love.
Breathe out from your center; imagine breathing
out love and sending it to All. To connect to the
love, peace of mind, and heart at your center, satu-
rate yourself with beauty and order. Beauty calms
the mind, opens the heart, and relaxes the body.
Now imagine that your breath carries life-giving
energy to some person or situation in your awareness. Breathe life-giving energy in and then breathe
it out. Open to receive love in whatever disguise
it might arrive. It may be in the form of support
from others or come as the mystery of synchronicity. As above, so below.

INQUIRY

What will my next breath create?

PRACTICE

Practice the above breath meditation.

I Am in a Good State of Practice

VERSE 93

I notice what I repeatedly experience and project, such as fear, judgment, appreciation, being stuck, anger, or frenzy. I examine my contribution to each experience, which reveals what is in shadow.

REFLECTION

Through a distorted lens, we often imagine fear where there is really nothing, direct judgment or anger where it does not belong, get stuck in struggle or move frantically to avoid the mirror. Life partners with us to co-create our experiences. If you wonder why some situations keep repeating, consider that life is a mirror of your inner world. What is of distortion creates separateness. What is of love creates Oneness, peace, and joy.

INQUIRY

What aspect of me do I see in the mirror of life?

PRACTICE

Notice when and where you are projecting.

Love and appreciate yourself even though you project this shadow. Own it as yours.

Ask, "What do I need to release this projection?"

Each day I take a risk, a good action that is
informed by my AWE Nature. I notice the cycle
and timing of events and initiate what is ripe
for beginning, nurture what is continuing,
and bring completion to each ending.

REFLECTION

Every day provides opportunities for good action.
A good action might be picking up the phone to
make a few calls or perhaps going to the beach.
Through the wisdom of AWE Nature, which is
always in connection with the big picture, you will
know what a good action could be. At times, life
asks for bold moves, actions that will shake the status quo of your sleepy comfort. Say yes for the sake
of expanding into the meaning and purpose of this
moment's calling. Risk is inherent in change. Either
you keep evolving through engaged presence and
action, or life may force your hand through unex-
pected bolts of lightning change.

INQUIRY

What is trying to happen in my life?

PRACTICE

Act on an inspiration that
takes courageous action.

I Am in a Good State of Practice

Each day I play, I laugh, I cry as a good
response to what is unfolding around me.

REFLECTION

There is no "right" emotional response to anything
that happens. Using the energy of AWE Nature,
your emotional response to life will be authentic,
well informed, balanced, and thus a good
response. As you fully experience all emotions,
your emotional field shifts accordingly. The emotion passes through as you process the experience.
Through distorted self, however, you may get stuck
in a particular emotion and recreate it over and
over by repeating your stories. Or you might avoid
the experience altogether. As a good response to
life, allow the emotion to pass through without an
agenda for taking a certain amount of time. Experience it fully.

INQUIRY

What emotion is moving through me now?

PRACTICE

What are you attached to?
What are you avoiding?
What is good? What will you do?

I Am in a Good State of Practice

I keep the agreements I make with others and myself.

REFLECTION

Let's meet for lunch! I'll call you sometime! We should get together! I'll have it ready tomorrow! All of these agreements, even made with good intention, create strings of energy and expectation. If the people involved follow through, then all is well. Too often, polite mutterings are just social graces that make it easy for people to say goodbye or avoid the real point. Eventually, this becomes a drag on your energy, clarity, and open heartedness. The same applies to agreements you make with yourself. If you say you will exercise tomorrow, you have promised a certain behavior. If you show up and follow through, then all is well. If not, in time you won't believe yourself anymore.

INQUIRY

What do I need for clean agreements?

PRACTICE

Notice your agreement habit. Is it clean and bright?

Do what is needed to make it so.

I Am in a Good State of Practice

I care for my relationships. Each day I reach
out and add value to the life of another.

REFLECTION

Even among the best of friends and family, there
is always the chance for misunderstanding. If we
continually avoid addressing such a mess, then the
communication gets clogged up. Relationships
are like gardens that require care and nurturing
from time to time. As a gardener, you have a great
opportunity each day to nurture your relationships
and bring them to a higher state of being. Engage
consciously in creating the quality of connection
you desire. This is important for all relationships,
including those with colleagues, neighbors, and
communities.

INQUIRY

What relationship needs my care now?

PRACTICE

If you have had a messy experience with someone
and the energy is still hanging out there, give the
person a call, have a conversation, and clean it up.

I Am in a Good State of Practice

A Good State of Doing

I am in a Good State of Doing.

VERSE 98
I do what is needed to live into the full expression of my being and purpose, such as developing my Self, talents, and skills and taking good action to become masterful at my calling.

VERSE 99
My body is the vehicle for action, my heart provides motivation, and my mind sets the direction. Therefore, my actions respect and honor the wholeness of my well-being.

VERSE 100
I gather the resources needed for success, including a circle of like-minded successful supporters.

VERSE 101
I am moving forward steadily, respecting the cycles and timing of the Universe around me.

VERSE 102
I recognize what must be done and will not go away, and I take care of it.

VERSE 103
I engage in at least one action each day that expresses my purpose in the world as well as I am able to interpret it.

VERSE 104

My actions are inspired through deep listening to the Universe, my heart's calling, and the wisdom of my AWE Nature.

VERSE 105

I take risks according to my AWE Nature's wisdom and move forward in a good way.

VERSE 106

I move in a conscious and intentional way when I act. I do so lightly with ease, delight, and good effort.

VERSE 107

I play and release my Self to the joyfulness of a child who, by blowing dandelion seed, releases and scatters joy to the world, then delights in the unfolding dream that each seed holds.

VERSE 108

I move as one—one of the people, one of many beings—so every breath, every action adds beauty and forwards the unfolding dream of the Universe in a good way.

I am in a Good State of Doing.

I do what is needed to live into the full expression of my being and purpose, such as developing my Self, talents, and skills and taking good action to become masterful at my calling.

REFLECTION

You were born with enough genius and talent to get by. That is, if coasting is what you imagine as the fullest expression of you in this amazing life. To really honor your gifts, you could instead practice and develop your Self to a world-class level. No matter what you are called to, it is beautiful to learn, grow, and develop your Self. As you do, you bring through joy and beauty as an inspiration to those around you. You are an instrument, and any instrument benefits from practice and tuning. Those who really lead the world usually work at it by developing themselves. Devotion to one's own talent honors the gift of this life.

INQUIRY

What would be possible if I practiced my talents?

PRACTICE

Commit to greatness and take action by practicing.

My body is the vehicle for action, my heart
provides motivation, my mind sets the
direction. Therefore, my actions respect and
honor the wholeness of my well-being.

REFLECTION

You have heard the expression that actions speak
louder than words. This is especially true when
it comes to personal well-being. Once you realize
that it is time to regain good health, it falls on
you to follow through. Commit to your intention. Many people "try" to do things. Trying is not
doing; it is just trying. If someone says he will try
to exercise, you might not expect anything to happen. The same applies when you tell yourself that
you will try. If you don't show up for yourself this
just erodes trust between you and your Self. Do or
don't do, but dismiss the state of trying. After you
have taken one action, it is important to be consis-
tent with further actions.

INQUIRY

What actions honor my well-being?

PRACTICE

Take one step today, one day
at a time, one life's journey.

I gather the resources needed for success, including a circle of like-minded successful supporters.

REFLECTION

Once you know what action is needed, gather the resources to support your success. Since ancient times, communities, churches, or other intentional circles would gather to be witness to someone called to action. Their role was to support with life-giving energy. Your job is to gather together such a group. If you already have a supportive circle, announce what you are up to and what you need from the group. If you do not have such a circle, call one together or join one that already exists. Be sure to empower the circle to hold you accountable and not collude with you in moments when you might shrink back from your call.

INQUIRY

Into what circle of support can I lean?

PRACTICE

Gather your circle and announce your intention. Design what is needed to support your success.

I am moving forward steadily, respecting the
cycles and timing of the Universe around me.

REFLECTION
Everything has a season, a cycle, and good timing.
Being aware of cycles allows your effort and action to be well directed for effective results. Burn-
out is the result of not respecting timing for your
own capacity or what is going on in the world. Is
your pace sustainable? Your action well timed?
Does this action respect your team and resources?
When action is driven by distortions (such as fear
of consequences) and untenable accountability
(without true buy-in), results are not sustainable.
Actions from AWE Nature are chosen wisely, well-
intended, engaged in with presence, held in good
accountability, and respectful of cycles and conditions of the world and those involved.

INQUIRY
In what season and cycle is my project?

PRACTICE
Notice where you are spinning your
wheels, pushing too hard, or not engaged.

What adjustments are wanted? Follow through.

I Am in a Good State of Doing

I recognize what must be done and will not go away, and I take care of it.

REFLECTION

As the saying goes, "Certain things will never go away, such as death and taxes." Other commitments are also here to stay. When you avoid doing something, the consequences of procrastinating may put a weight on your energy, time, and resources. There is no freedom in avoiding. Learn to recognize which matters are important and how to take care of them in a good way. The freedom that results from meeting your obligations will set mind and heart free. As well, choose to do fun, delightful things that are equally good for your well-being and give them high priority, such as going on regular holidays, walks, date nights, and so on.

INQUIRY

What obligation nags for my attention?

PRACTICE

Be clear about essential tasks and do at least one action a day to address them.

I Am in a Good State of Doing

I engage in at least one action each day
that expresses my purpose in the world
as well as I am able to interpret it.

REFLECTION

"Pay yourself first" is an adage in the world of personal finances. The idea is that with each check earned, you put aside a portion as an investment in your future. This works equally well for setting aside time for yourself—creating your dream, fulfilling your purpose, writing a book, or doing other important projects. Each day, engage in one action that furthers your life purpose. This could be one phone call, one chapter, or one act of kindness. The rest of the day is available for other choices, including play. Of course, some days will be more productive than others. But you will be amazed at how much can be accomplished one day at a time.

INQUIRY

What action does a project want from me today?

PRACTICE

Take one action today on that important project. Engage in that action with ease and delight.

I Am in a Good State of Doing

VERSE 104

My actions are inspired through deep
listening to the Universe, my heart's calling,
and the wisdom of my AWE Nature.

REFLECTION

Have you ever found yourself going through the motions of a task in which you are barely present to what you are doing or why? We have all had those days. Some routine jobs need doing and don't require much creativity. In a fulfilling life and career, we are presented with opportunities that challenge us and tap into our creative genius. If this is not happening, perhaps the Universe is trying to get your attention. Restlessness, intuition, or others' insights could be asking you to consider expressing your talents in different ways than you are now. Notice what you would rather be doing as a clue.

INQUIRY

What is the Universe asking of me?

PRACTICE

Notice feedback regarding what would
be a good use of you and your talents
at this time in your life.

Listen deeply. Experiment with your genius.

VERSE 105

I take risks according to my AWE Nature's wisdom and move forward in a good way.

REFLECTION

One day long ago, I was living a great life. I was happy, successful, and on a good path. I awoke one morning feeling deeply stirred with a new calling. I knew in my core that this yearning would put my world at risk. I had a lot to lose it seemed. I chose to trust that the calling was more important than the circumstances of my happy, prosperous life. I was being asked to step away from the scaffolding I had created, no matter how wonderful it all seemed. I set off with no plan—only trust mixed with fear. I had no idea where the adventure would take me. I didn't know what I didn't know; but my heart did know possibilities. Guided by intuition and willingness to listen deeply to wisdom, to my heart, I let go.

INQUIRY

What stirs within?

PRACTICE

Notice what you are holding onto.
Notice what stirs you from within. Act.

I Am in a Good State of Doing

VERSE 106

I move in a conscious and intentional
way when I act. I do so lightly with
ease, delight, and good effort.

REFLECTION

One day walking though the Himalayas, we faced
a long, steep, upward climb. The trail mocked our
weariness with a dare and a challenge. My companions projected anger at each other. I felt a pull
to join them in this suffering. I realized that, as
with any other mountain in life, we could choose
to climb or turn away. I could also choose to walk
with anger or joy. I chose joy. Grace guided me to
the top in no time, for delight is not constrained
by time. My companions were nowhere in sight,
so I went back down. I offered, and one allowed
me, to carry her pack. On the way back up, once
again I in-joyed the journey. I made four trips up
the mountain that day. Later at the top, freed from
anger and suffering, we all cried as we took in the
beauty of humanity through each other.

INQUIRY

In what way will I engage in action today?

PRACTICE

Experiment by choosing different energies.

I Am in a Good State of Doing

VERSE 107

I play and I release my Self to the joyfulness of
a child who, by blowing dandelion seed, releases
and scatters joy to the world, then delights in
the unfolding dream that each seed holds.

REFLECTION

There is within all of us a magical child who, given
the chance, would love to come out and play. As
a kid, I loved fast cars. I used to walk the neigh-
borhood and hang out at the local garage just to
see what the older guys were driving. We had a
motorized go-cart, and I would drive the neighbors
crazy zooming up and down the streets. At eight
years old, I would get pulled over by the police,
who were quite sympathetic about the dilemma
of where to drive my cart. Racing that cart around
brought me great delight. Now as an adult, I love
to go to the track, rent a cart, and let that little boy
within have a day of pure joy.

INQUIRY

What play would my inner child love today?

PRACTICE

Take your inner child out for an adventure.

VERSE 108

I move as one—one of the people, one of
many beings—so every breath, every action
adds beauty and forwards the unfolding
dream of the Universe in a good way.

REFLECTION

Any idea that leads you to experience distortion—
fear, doubt, criticism, judgment, shame, blame,
feeling less or better than—is an illusion, a lie. If
you dare to peek behind the curtain of the lie you
started believing oh so long ago, you will be confronted with the truth of your beauty. It is now
time to snap out of the delusion of unworthiness
and live into the fullness of life. We are all broth-
ers and sisters, fathers and mothers, neighbors and
community members who are in the same unfolding dream together. In my dream, I wish you
an experience of your own beauty, love, and life-
giving energy.

INQUIRY

What is possible if I choose to
be and act in love today?

PRACTICE

As you move among people, create
an action that gives lift to another.

I Am in a Good State of Doing

Conclusion

As I write, I am guiding a vision quest in the Joshua Tree desert region of Southern California. I am in awe of the amazing people who have gathered here. Each has come for his or her own personal reasons, and every one is generously supporting the others toward their visions, healing, and the gathering of wisdom about what is next in life.

I wonder what it would be like if everyone on earth would have the courage to engage in developing so fully and beautifully. What if we all were willing to set aside the illusion of busyness, scarcity, importance, unworthiness, or whatever else drives us? What if we opened our hearts and minds to growth? The world could be so different if we engaged in human development for the sake of a better life, experience, prosperity, and deeper relationships with Self, the land, and each other.

It is my hope that by playing with the ideas expressed here, you will find your way to a richer, more vibrant life experience. If you take on the spirit of this work, adjust as needed so it is personally relevant, and apply yourself according to a good state of effort and intention, you will certainly experience a great shift toward happiness, peace, creativity, and fulfillment.

As we each raise our consciousness and adapt our behavior accordingly, we have a positive impact on those around us. You are a point of light shining the way for all. Thank you for holding your part of the web.

The Eight States of an Awakened Life™

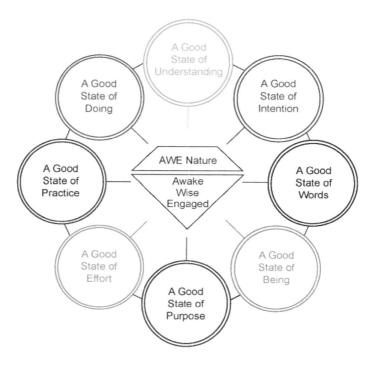

Full list of verses

I am in a Good State of Understanding.

VERSE 1

I understand that All and I are interrelated, and as such we are One.

VERSE 2

I seek understanding.

VERSE 3

I am infinite consciousness; I am the sweeper of the broom; I am the mirror; I am you; I am who I aspire to be; I am the inspired and the inspiration.

VERSE 4

I understand that as a human, I aspire, learn, grow, and develop throughout this human journey and that there is no such destination as perfection or finished.

VERSE 5

I understand that we are all part of the Wisdom Field.

VERSE 6

I understand that the true nature of this Universe is diversity. I respect the value of the full range of beings, things, and ideas that make up the wholeness of this Universe.

VERSE 7

I understand that my expectations, intentions, and words are powerful tools of creation.

VERSE 8

I understand that I am my own healer. The healing and balancing activity of my mind, body, and heart is a constant process.

VERSE 9

I understand that what I believe to be absolutely true becomes true because I believe it. Therefore, I understand that holding a question is more useful than grasping an answer.

VERSE 10

I understand that I am the self-authority of the whole of my life, and it is through my choices that I author the unfolding adventure.

VERSE 11

I understand that All is energy, that energy just is, and that energy is transformed according to the intentions of my thoughts, words, and actions.

VERSE 12

I understand that I create my own karma. Every intention, thought, word, or action has an impact, and every impact has a consequence for which I am responsible.

VERSE 13

I understand that we are learning and developing through this life, and so I meet us All with generosity, compassion, and good intention.

VERSE 14

I understand that all people, beings, things, and circumstances are impermanent and there is a natural cycle and timing to All. Thus, the opportunity of each moment is to be present, for past and future live only as story or dream, and the moment of now is where all is One.

VERSE 15

I understand the Law of Attraction: whatever I put my expectation and intention on is what I will create in my life. I am in a dance with the Universe. What I call in, therefore, will be in accordance with the larger unfolding picture of All.

VERSE 16

I understand that this Universe is generous in its nature, abundant in possibilities, and filled with all the resources that all beings and I need.

I am in a Good State of Intention.

VERSE 17

I am open and responding to the call, today's expression of my being, and I develop myself willingly to be what I am.

VERSE 18

My intention is informed by my dream, vision, and purpose. It is in resonance with my own wisdom as inspired through my heart-mind-body connection to the Wisdom Field.

VERSE 19

I meet all others and myself with love, generosity, and compassion. I create a respectful space for our commonality and diversity, for well-being and the wholeness in which we are One.

VERSE 20
I meet the challenge of obstacles and opportunities that appear along my path with the intention of learning, growing, appreciating, and loving all that shows up.

VERSE 21
From a Good State of Intention, my thoughts arise. This stream of consciousness carries beauty and life-giving energy out to all beings who are touched by her waters.

VERSE 22
I notice each thought as it arises and choose whether or not to encourage it, feed it, fan its embers. If through discernment I decide that a thought does not add beauty or is not life giving, then I release it.

VERSE 23
My intentions burn bright with love and the willingness to be generous with my time, effort, and resources to all beings and myself.

VERSE 24
I am tolerant and curious with those I do not understand. I am also compassionate with the fearful, judgmental, doubtful aspects of my own self. I realize that any sense of other, or separation, is of my own making. Therefore, I hold the intention

and willingness to remove any veils of separation that exist as I touch into the Oneness, which we all are.

I am in a Good State of Words.

VERSE 25
Sound creates transformation. I am the instrument of sound through tones, hymns, chants, affirmations, prayer, song, and words—according to the wisdom of my AWE Nature.

VERSE 26
I tell the stories as this day's expression of who I am, allowing my state of wholeness to be beyond description.

VERSE 27
My words are informed by the inspiration, vision, and dream of the Universe's call; they resonate with the One heartbeat.

VERSE 28
My words are created from my Good State of Intention; therefore, my speech creates beauty and more life.

VERSE 29
My words honor all those around me, including myself.

VERSE 30
My words reflect my inner state of being.

VERSE 31
My words create positive effects on those who hear them and those about whom I speak.

VERSE 32
My words are not used as a weapon against others or myself.

VERSE 33
My words evoke creativity, generosity, appreciation, and good action.

VERSE 34
My words are carried by breath, which blows encouragement onto the embers of possibility for others and myself.

VERSE 35
My words are spoken cleanly in challenging situations, and I listen, listen, listen.

VERSE 36
My words give life to what desires to be born and completion to what is ready to let go.

VERSE 37
My words are truthful, kind, and needed.

I am in a Good State of Being.

VERSE 38
I am Source and living as One with all.

VERSE 39

I am who I choose to be in this day's expression of the wholeness that I am.

VERSE 40

I regard all people, beings, and situations with the humility of one who meets a reflection of Universal beauty.

VERSE 41

Because I am in a Good State of Being, my spirit is bright and joyous.

VERSE 42

I am in right relationship with the Wisdom Field; therefore, I listen and respond according to the guidance of my AWE Nature.

VERSE 43

When I am experiencing discord with the wisdom of my AWE Nature, I look into the cause and ask what is needed. I then respond and follow through.

VERSE 44

Because I am in a Good State of Being, I am the source of my joy.

VERSE 45

I am in right relationship with my three wisdom portals—body, heart, and mind.

VERSE 46

I am in right relationship with my body; therefore, I treat my body with kindness, good food, exercise, and care.

VERSE 47

I am in right relationship with my heart and therefore check in often with my emotions. I activate my heart wisdom.

VERSE 48

I am in right relationship with my mind and therefore practice discernment of word and thought always.

VERSE 49

I love my shadow and the wholeness of my being.

VERSE 50

I am in right relationship with the earth and all beings, including the plants, animals, minerals, soil, waters, and every other aspect of earth and the surrounding Uni-verse.

VERSE 51

I am a beacon of light that shines loving-kindness for all, including myself.

VERSE 52

I live in trust of myself and therefore move forward in a good way.

VERSE 53

I am a lifelong learner. I allow myself to risk succeeding or failing and to learn always.

I am in a Good State of Purpose.

VERSE 54

I am beyond the box that would allow only one stated purpose. I willingly commit to my highest expression of purpose each day.

VERSE 55

I embrace the gift of this precious life and the opportunity to be—sensually, emotionally, and mindfully—all that is in accordance with my AWE Wisdom.

VERSE 56

I am well used as I stay present to my experience.

VERSE 57

I am not attached to any particular direction on my path; therefore, I am available to my vision, my purpose, and the dream Universe.

VERSE 58

I honor the gift of this life, and I unfold my purpose daily according to my AWE Nature.

VERSE 59

I understand that the ultimate purpose of this precious life is a great mystery.

VERSE 60

I author my moment-by-moment unfolding as I dance with the emerging story of the Universe.

VERSE 61

I allow my purpose to emerge from each Now moment; therefore, I remain open to the call of my AWE Nature and the Universe.

VERSE 62

According to my wisdom, I live beyond unconscious, limiting expectations and willingly take risks to expand myself and the well-being of All.

VERSE 63

Our purposes are interrelated; therefore, I am available to support you and others as we fulfill life's call.

VERSE 64

I am in a Good State of Purpose; therefore, my livelihood honors the values of my AWE Nature.

VERSE 65

My success is not measured by the size or results of my efforts but by the beauty that comes from how I respond in each passing moment.

VERSE 66

I unfold my purpose simply through each breath and sweep of the broom.

VERSE 67

In each moment, I am in-joy and on purpose in a good way.

I am in a Good State of Effort.

VERSE 68

I apply good effort each day to allow my call to be

expressed according to the inspiration received through wisdom.

VERSE 69

Because I am in a Good State of Effort, I am mindful in each moment.

VERSE 70

I hold effort and mindfulness with commitment, beauty, ease, delight, and flow.

VERSE 71

As I am at choice, I apply my will to follow through and move forward according to my choice.

VERSE 72

My problems are just challenges that invite me to engage in a good way.

VERSE 73

I am flexible, allowing my emotions, stories, and beliefs to shift in accordance with my growth and the wisdom of my AWE Nature.

VERSE 74

When I want someone or something around me to be different, I apply the right measure of effort to be responsible and to become that myself first.

VERSE 75

I apply good effort to remember my genius, talents, and gifts and to be mindful of the stories I repeat about myself.

VERSE 76

I attend to what is needed with wisdom rather than aversion, attraction, or attachment.

VERSE 77

I apply the right measure of energy to follow through and complete what I intend—with ease, delight, and respect for cycles and timing. I apply my will in a good way.

VERSE 78

I apply the effort of appreciation for every being and situation I have attracted to my life. Releasing judgment, I apply good effort to recover to openness, listening, curiosity, and understanding.

VERSE 79

I am actively compassionate and forgiving to all, including myself.

VERSE 80

I honor cycles and timing, remaining at choice about when to act and when to be still.

VERSE 81

I look into each moment and ask what is needed. I respond with the wisdom of my AWE Nature.

VERSE 82

I accept that life will have many beginnings and endings, successes and failings. Every day is a good day to begin again.

I am in a Good State of Practice.

VERSE 83
I practice and develop the art of expressing my being, values, and purpose daily.

VERSE 84
Each day I check in with my inner and outer experience, my state of being.

VERSE 85
I create my day consciously and care for my state of being.

VERSE 86
I plan my day according to AWE Nature's wisdom. I am intentional and flexible as the mystery in each moment unfolds.

VERSE 87
I care daily for my physical body, mind, emotional body, and spirit.

VERSE 88
In each day, I have a time of stillness. I listen to the beating of my heart, to my breath, and to the call of the Universe.

VERSE 89
Each day I meditate.

VERSE 90
I consciously express love and appreciate all that shows up in the unfolding of my journey, including the things that seem unpleasant or inconvenient.

VERSE 91

I check in with the Wisdom Field each day and ask what is needed. I listen and respond according to my AWE Nature.

VERSE 92

Each day I create internal beauty; I breathe in love. I create beauty and order in the space around me; I breathe out love and send life-giving energy to all beings.

VERSE 93

I notice what I repeatedly experience and project, such as fear, judgment, appreciation, being stuck, anger, or frenzy. I examine my contribution to each experience, which reveals what is in shadow.

VERSE 94

Each day I take a risk, a good action that is informed by my AWE Nature. I notice the cycle and timing of events and initiate what is ripe for beginning, nurture what is continuing, and bring completion to each ending.

VERSE 95

Each day I play, I laugh, I cry as a good response to what is unfolding around me.

VERSE 96

I keep the agreements I make with others and myself.

VERSE 97

I care for my relationships. Each day I reach out and add value to the life of another.

I am in a Good State of Doing.

VERSE 98

I do what is needed to live into the full expression of my being and purpose, such as developing my self, talents, and skills and taking good action to become masterful at my calling.

VERSE 99

My body is the vehicle for action, my heart provides motivation, and my mind sets the direction. Therefore, my actions respect and honor the wholeness of my well-being.

VERSE 100

I gather the resources needed for success, including a circle of like-minded successful supporters.

VERSE 101

I am moving forward steadily, respecting the cycles and timing of the Universe around me.

VERSE 102

I recognize what must be done and will not go away, and I take care of it.

VERSE 103

I engage in at least one action each day that expresses my purpose in the world as well as I am able to interpret it.

VERSE 104

My actions are inspired through deep listening to the Universe, my heart's calling, and the wisdom of my AWE Nature.

VERSE 105

I take risks according to my AWE Nature's wisdom and move forward in a good way.

VERSE 106

I move in a conscious and intentional way when I act. I do so lightly with ease, delight, and good effort.

VERSE 107

I play and release my Self to the joyfulness of a child who, by blowing dandelion seed, releases and scatters joy to the world, then delights in the unfolding dream that each seed holds.

VERSE 108

I move as one—one of the people, one of many beings—so every breath, every action adds beauty and forwards the unfolding dream of the Universe in a good way.

In his own words . . . *"Corporations, organizations and individuals often reach out for coaching and guidance during times of great transition. While those moments can often be perceived as painful or difficult, they also offer the best opportunities to move forward into our core purpose and highest potential. Life is never predictable nor within our control. I have learned when to take my hands off the wheel and when to steer, and to remain responsive to the day-by-day unfolding of life and the call. I am privileged to work with entrepreneurs, executives, teams, vision questers and creatives in very powerful ways. I engage with people supporting, provoking and shining light onto their journeys as they navigate through both mundane and profound life decisions."*

Patrick J. Ryan has travelled the world speaking and leading workshops in 15 different countries to thousands of people and worked with audiences from 10 to 1,000 participants on the importance of leading with impact. As a former Buddhist monk in Burma (now Myanmar), Patrick practiced the path of awakened living and uses all of his teachings and experiences in his role as executive coach, leadership trainer, bestselling author and founder of Awakened Wisdom Experiences™ Inc.

Patrick works with executives and entrepreneurs, focusing on questions of personal effectiveness, development, transformation and leadership. Powerfully integrating his life experiences with ancient teachings and modern applications, Patrick coaches his clients to more deeply understand and integrate all of their experiences and wisdom to propel them to their highest goals.

Patrick has more than twenty-five years of proven experience as a senior trainer for coaches and creating Leadership Development Programs and Vision Quests. Learn more about Patrick and how to work with him at www.AwakenedWisdom.com.

Awakened Wisdom Retreats and Programs

The following represents a few of the offerings available from Awakened Wisdom Experiences. Please check our website www.AwakenedWisdom.com for additional offerings and for details on these programs.

VISION QUESTS

Join Patrick in the ancient tradition of the Vision Quest. Allow a space and time to examine your life; tap into a source of renewal, creativity and vitality. Join our scheduled nature-based retreats, or book your own private leadership Vision Quest—for yourself, community or organization.

COACHING SERVICES

Are you on the edge leading your organization, deep in a life transition, or facing a radical change in career or life situation? Or, do you just want to find out more about who you are and discover more of your genius and talent, and ways to bring that through your career and life more fully? Patrick's Personal and Executive coach services provide guidance and direction, to help you refine your goals and life Purpose, and to clarify your vision.

AWE Nature Coaching(SM) is offered exclusively by Awakened Wisdom Experiences Inc. authorized coaches.

CORPORATE RETREATS

AWE Corporate retreats provide the space and time for you and your organization to hone your goals and mission and to develop a strategy to pursue success. Awakened Wisdom offers a variety of training opportunities: Leadership and Talent Development, Coaching Skills for Leadership, Team Relationship Enhancement, In-house Coach Training.

COACHING SKILLS FOR LEADERSHIP

For more than 30 years, Patrick has been successfully teaching, training and coaching entrepreneurs, educators, corporate leaders, and people of all ages, cultures and backgrounds to create the life and results they desire. These principals are seamlessly applied to the work environment to create motivated teams, develop and manage top talent, and to navigate through conflict or change with ease and strength.

TRAINING FOR COACHES

Whether you are an experienced coach or someone using coaching skills in your profession, Awakened Wisdom training will deepen your practice and create even more vibrancy and power in your coaching and communications. This is a powerful program. Patrick has created a solid foundation for grounding clients in AWE Nature™ and self-awareness for the sake of coaching them to success.

Visit our website at www.AwakenedWisdom.com.